MANAGING WITHOUT CONFLICT

by

Will Clark

MANAGING WITHOUT CONFLICT

**How To Create
Extraordinary Productivity
By Eliminating
Ordinary Conflict**

© 2010 by Will Clark

ISBN 145288823X

Motivation Basics
P.O. Box 6327
Diamondhead, MS 39525
228-255-5019

For More Information Visit The Author At
AuthorsDen.com

CONTENTS

Managing The Conflict Zone

PREFACE

Since the beginning of modern leadership in the early 1900s, leaders remain frustrated and puzzled over the question of how to increase productivity. The need for productivity and motivational concerns became prominent during the industrial revolution, which introduced mass production with the interchangeability of parts. Initially, it was assumed that money and fear were the logical motivators.

This question became even more complex after the 1930s, when it was suggested by research that for workers to be productive they might be influenced by factors that are more personal than simply economic and financial gain. The human relations approach to leadership weakened the concept that pay and salary were enough to motivate workers. This approach, however, also generated more questions than it answered. The dominant question of the human relations approach concerns how to achieve effective worker motivation.

This book isn't designed as a total thesis on motivation. There are many other writings that analyze that subject. This book, however, recognizes and considers those motivation ideas and concepts to demonstrate that workplace conflict is the major force that defeats those motivational attempts. Even the greatest motivator, or the greatest motivational technique, will fail in the workplace if conflict in that workplace isn't eliminated, or at least reduced to a minimum level.

The information in this book shows how to eliminate that conflict to allow valid motivation efforts to be effective in one's efforts to increase productivity and success.

Managing The Conflict Zone

INTRODUCTION

The ultimate goal of a business organization is survival. Coincidental with that goal an organization serves many purposes, some of which are related to that goal and some aren't. Some related purposes include profit, growth, power, and security for company leaders or owners. Some indirect purposes include economic growth of society, governmental stability and opportunities for individuals to develop personal careers.

Some organizations accomplish their goal of survival while others do not. Survival or failure of a company may be attributed to many different reasons, many of which include the following:

- An erroneous business concept

- Inadequate financing

- Lack of business skills

- Lack of sufficient demand

- Lack of interest and enthusiasm

- The wrong marketing approach

- The wrong business location

- Poor leadership

- Unskilled or unmotivated workers

This list of typical reasons for business failures includes those that may be somewhat identified as a business begins to decline. For example, it's relatively easy to determine if a business is not financed adequately, for funds will be lacking to make current payments; it's relatively easy to know if the wrong marketing approach is being used by comparing results with other similar businesses; and, it's certainly easy to know if the demand for a product or service is inadequate.

More difficult to identify are those failures related to personnel quality, enthusiasm, skills, and effort. These are usually difficult to identify and isolate as a basic problem, for they're usually vaguely intertwined and camouflaged by other more visible problems. Furthermore, personnel problems tend to adjust to defend themselves by blaming other problems.

For example, weak or incompetent leaders may ordinarily blame bad luck, lazy workers, or inadequate support for their lack of effectiveness. Lazy workers may ordinarily blame unfair company policies, unfair work schedules, or bad leadership for their lack of productivity. In either case, it's difficult to understand exactly what the cause really is when inefficiency is caused by people in the workplace. That determination is usually made from the perspective of the person who's responsible for that productivity.

Most problems in a workplace, assuming that the business is established on valid business principles, are caused by people. If a business has the right concept, is in the right location, and has sufficient demand for that product or service, then the basics are there for that company to survive and be profitable. The determining factor of that business success then becomes the effort of the people charged with making that business profitable.

Ordinarily, it's a simple task to find capable and qualified people to perform those functions to make a business survive. Most people in society are normal people with average intelligence. Most jobs in society don't require people to have superior intelligence; therefore, when trained workers are available to perform those jobs.

Leadership positions are more difficult to fill. The concept of leadership is so vague it's often difficult to be confident that a person hired to be a leader will actually be an effective leader. This uncertainty exists even though that leader might have been an outstanding leader in another organization. The effectiveness of a leader is more often evaluated from the leader's results than from the characteristics and traits a leader exhibits. Those results are often determined by influences outside the leader's direct control.

These contributing forces that determine the effectiveness of leadership may be identified as workplace harmony or workplace conflict. The level of workplace conflict in an organization usually determines if leaders are considered competent, if workers are considered skilled, and if that workplace will achieve its highest level of efficient productivity.

Many books, magazine articles, newspaper articles, theses, and other documents have been written to guide leaders in the art of leadership to increase productivity. These writings have focused primarily at two subjects: improving leadership skills and learning to motivate workers.

Two fundamental problems exist with these training targets. First, a scientific leadership model doesn't exist to permit positive leadership training. Secondly, motivation theories are only vague theories, they aren't based on fact. Consequently, that training is based on ideas and concepts, not proven models.

Even if one accepts the idea that leadership and motivation training is valid, one must also change the target of that training. Current targets are: improving leadership skills and improving worker motivation. The single target of leadership training should be simply to eliminate workplace conflict. Of course, further explanation is necessary to grasp this concept. This concept is based on existing leadership and motivation theories.

There is no single leadership style that produces uniform productivity results. In some situations, autocratic leaders may have more productive workplaces than democratic leaders. In other situations democratic leaders might get more positive results.

Although leadership styles are categorized basically as autocratic or democratic, most leaders function somewhere between those two extremes. A totally autocratic leader or a totally democratic leader probably doesn't exist. Normally the democratic style is preferred, for it offers workers more freedom from stress and more opportunities to become motivated.

Motivation theories suggest, imply, or openly state that motivation occurs naturally. These motivation theories are based on the premise that people are moved to action to satisfy needs. Based on these theories everyone must be motivated to do something since everyone has some needs.

A synthesis of these ideas of leadership and motivation suggests a conclusion that leaders shouldn't focus merely on leadership skills and motivation in the workplace. Instead, leaders should focus on eliminating conflict in the workplace to allow workers to unleash their internal and withheld self motivation to fill their natural achievement needs, meaningful work, and recognition. This book is designed for this leadership purpose.

This book is designed to accomplish two other fundamental purposes, other than to demonstrate how to eliminate conflict to increase productivity. It's also designed to give a brief but comprehensive leadership course, and to introduce a simple personal success planning guide for leaders and workers.

Personal success planning by workers is introduced to establish the concept that a worker who's focused on personal development will be less vulnerable to distracting negative influences. These distracting negative influences are often the catalysts to conflict that reduces productivity in a workplace.

1

CONFLICT DIMENSIONS

Any organization, particularly a business organization, exists for two fundamental purposes. First is simply for survival of the organization, although that might not have been the intent of the organization upon its inception. The second is that of production, usually intended to result in a financial profit. There are some non-profitable and charitable organizations that might not be designed for personal profit, but they, nevertheless, are designed for an identifiable form of productivity.

Productivity, whether designed for profit or non-profit, is determined by a myriad of conditions and factors. These factors include such variables as: level of technology, marketing strategies, skill level of competitors, availability of resources, financial arrangements, transportation sources, storage and distribution capabilities, product demand, leadership abilities, and worker performance. The integration of these important factors ultimately determines the survival and profitability of an organization.

In most organizations the least measurable and the most burdensome of these factors is the quality of leaders and workers; and more specifically, the relationship between leaders and workers. These important relationships are ultimately determined by the conflict that exists between those leaders and workers. A low level of conflict allows leaders and workers to have higher concentration and focus on the purpose of the organization - productivity. A high level of conflict becomes focused on itself and, consequently, detracts from productivity goals.

Workplace conflict has only two basic sources. Even with only two sources, however, the real cause of conflict is rarely determined; or in many cases if the cause is determined it may be ignored. The source of workplace conflict is usually ignored if that source is the leader. The other source of conflict is workers. Workers usually are blamed as the source of workplace conflict regardless of the real source, since leaders ordinarily determine the source of conflict.

Ordinarily, conflict doesn't become a question unless the level of productivity in an organization is questioned. Conflict may also be created through clashes of individual personalities. These dimensions of conflict in work environments will be examined next.

Dimensions Of Conflict

Conflict exists in most, if not all, business organizations. It would be rare if an organization existed without having some conflict. The level of conflict ordinarily is self-evident, but there are many conditions where that conflict is latent and seething and doesn't show itself with signs of open hostility. This subtle conflict would be exhibited by worker lethargy, increased accidents, and unexplained mistakes. These incidents would be misinterpreted as lack of motivation, lack of attention, or lack of ability. Although these would be the visible signs, ordinarily latent conflict would be the basic source of those problems.

It's generally believed that conflict that creates productivity problems in an organization exists only between leaders and workers. Most writings that concern workplace conflict imply this is the only dimension of conflict. There are, however, four dimensions of conflict in most business organizations, or other workplaces. These four dimensions may be identified by the acronym BUMS, which include:

B - Bottom level workers

U - Upper level managers

M - Middle managers

S - Supervisors

Each of these dimensions will be analyzed individually, beginning at the top level of management. This analysis will descend through the hierarchy from the top.

Upper-level Management

Conflict exists at the highest levels of an organization. This conflict is created by conditions and decisions within the senior group, between the senior group and industry expectations and between that level and middle managers.

Ordinarily, there are personality clashes and strong differences of opinion within the senior group that echo down through the entire organization to create more ambivalence and conflict at lower levels. Even when personality clashes don't exist, there are usually situations of jockeying and positioning for more personal power and control for increased personal esteem and status. These activities cannot fail to be influences that create negative reactions at lower levels. People at lower levels resent top leaders who try to become more powerful by ignoring those more important survival needs at those lower levels.

Some conflict also exists between the desires of top leaders and the expectations and demands of their industry and their company charters. These conflicts place restrictions on top leaders that don't allow them to make decisions they would otherwise make. These limitations also place restrictions on their individual efforts to gain more personal power.

The relationship between senior managers and middle managers is also another normal source of conflict. Unless those relationships are close, based upon longstanding friendships, each level of management has its own priorities, perspectives, and biases. Top managers who have less direct control over the productivity process often forget that real people are really involved in that productivity process.

Top management's plans and programs are ordinarily based upon quotas, percentage of profit increase, price of stock, and other factors that affect their esteem; things outside the process of actually influencing productivity workers to accomplish productivity tasks. If they are too far removed from the reality of the productivity process, their plans and directions conflict with the normal abilities of lower-level leaders to sustain those levels. The resulting tension and stress eventually produce alienation and frustration.

Middle Managers

Conflict ordinarily increases as it moves downward in an organization. Middle managers become trapped in an area that doesn't permit clear alternative actions or answers. They must accomplish their tasks, usually without serious questioning, to demonstrate their personal loyalty to their senior leader, regardless of the motives or the competency of that leader. They must also comply with those policies that often create conflict to allow themselves to remain competitive for promotions and advancements. This conflict creates even more stress and discomfort if the demands and expectations are too high for an indefinite time, especially if the management styles of the two leaders aren't compatible.

A human relations manager who's accountable to an autocratic senior leader; or a more autocratic subordinate leader who reports to a human relations oriented leader will have difficulty communicating

14

with each other. That lack of common perceptions will not allow them to develop mutual policies. The subordinate leader becomes tense, stressed, and ambivalent, all of which are conditions that cause conflict.

Subordinate leaders, middle managers, are also in natural conflict with supervisors who report to them. This natural conflict springs from two basic sources. First is the conflict created by the belief by many of those supervisors that their managers don't have enough influence with higher leaders to prevent undue pressure and exploitation of themselves and their workers.

The second source of conflict is that produced by the need of both to have enough influence and authority to fulfill their normal esteem needs. Often the duties of middle managers and supervisors are ambiguous and overlap; which creates resentment and hesitancy to communicate freely and openly. For example, many supervisors feel the manager should not communicate directly with workers without 'going through' the supervisor. Often, in fact, managers purposefully avoid communicating through the supervisor to develop a feeling of being closer to the action.

Supervisors

The pressure for conflict continues to increase as it moves further down the hierarchal chain in the organization. Since supervisors are ordinarily at the bottom of the authority hierarchy, the pressure for conflict is greatest at that level. Not only have the ambiguities, the fears, the apprehensions, and the incompetence been passed down through each level of the organization, the supervisor must guide multi-faceted workers with all this excess baggage that's been channeled downward.

The supervisor is not free to guide workers on a one-on-one level. The supervisor must also filter out those dictates and guidelines that would cause negative reactions from the workers; while at the same time, try to make it appear to higher leadership that all those policies and guidelines were, in fact, enforced.

The supervisor must also consider his or her career and esteem needs to find a comfortable position that will maintain a reasonable level of productivity. At the same time the supervisor must attempt to satisfy the productivity and esteem needs of superiors in the company. Again, this task is more difficult and complicated if the leadership styles of the supervisor and the middle manager are conflicting.

A supervisor who must function under the leadership of an autocratic manager is certainly at a great disadvantage in trying to create harmonious and productive relationships with his or her workers. Ordinarily, conflict at this level will not allow harmonious relationships at the working level. Productivity might be maintained for a time by using fear, intimidation, and threats. Productivity will not result from normal worker motivation.

Supervisors have a greater potential for conflict than do higher levels of management for another important reason; that is, conflict in ideologies. All managers, including supervisors, are normally trained in the concepts and principles of management. Some supervisors receive less training than others, but even those who aren't as well trained or indoctrinated still accept the responsibility of leadership. This acceptance of responsibility becomes a shift in ideology and values. Responsibility and direct accountability place inherent pressure to accomplish tasks and assignments.

Regardless of one's level of interest or competency as a worker, when that worker becomes a leader those ideologies will shift. For example, a union shop steward might suddenly see the disasters caused by unions when he or she becomes promoted to a company supervisor. This shift in ideology from the worker level contains inherent conflict.

Workers

The pressure for conflict continues to bulge as it moves downward to the last link in the hierarchal chain. Workers are the last link in that chain. They, too, face many sources of potential conflict. The first source of conflict for workers is their relationship with the supervisor. It doesn't matter if the supervisor is one who uses the autocratic style or the human relations leadership style, conflict still exists. An autocratic leader, naturally, will almost always incite and generate conflict regardless of the quality of workers. On the other hand, some workers will resent any authority, even from a supervisor who attempts to gain productivity without using direct and forceful authority. This reaction may have three causes: (1) the personality of the worker, (2) peer pressure and, (3) a dislike of the company or company policies.

The second source of conflict at the worker level results from the necessity to work with other workers who have different personalities, goals, aspirations, and cultural backgrounds. Workers, ordinarily, cannot choose their peers. They must work with others without consideration of individual personalities. The concept of having to work equally with one who's considered of lower cultural or social status is a direct attack upon one's esteem and self-image. Since esteem is usually the strongest personal motivator, this direct attack creates negative reactions that may eventually cause conflict.

The third source of conflict at the worker level is that of alternatives. Most workers work because they must, not because they want to. Many young workers also work at jobs they consider inferior and only temporary. They plan to 'get a better job' or 'go to school' one day. Since the job is not serious to them at the time, many other more desirable activities distract them from becoming fully motivated to focus on the demands of the job. This lack of concern and focus normally results in conflict with productivity expectations of the supervisor.

The fourth source of conflict for workers is the insensitivity of leaders to consider personal problems. Many young workers have problems that leaders and more mature workers often forget when they reach those higher and more stable levels of the maturation process.

Young workers often have children who become ill or have accidents; young workers are often nurtured in culturally deprived backgrounds and aren't aware of the necessity for good nutrition to avoid illness; young workers often cannot afford reliable transportation; and, young workers are rarely trained in the process of self-development for success. They are usually trained only just enough to be technically competent on the job. Then they're expected to learn how to be a successful worker and a successful person, accidentally, by themselves. Most likely, this lack of concern for personal development of workers is the basis for organized labor's flag word of *exploitation*.

The fifth source of conflict at the worker level in an organization is alienation. The stronger and more universal is this feeling of alienation by a worker, the more susceptible that worker becomes to normal frustrations and conflicts. Alienation of workers may be more than just a simple feeling in the workplace, it may also become a lifestyle that generates further frustrations and despair.

Ordinarily, workers who understand the success process and have a success plan for themselves don't become vulnerable to alienation. A self-development process helps to keep one in control of his or her destiny by allowing that person to be in the driver's seat, instead of lurking silently in the back seat wondering where the driver is going. Unfortunately, most workers don't have a success plan for themselves. They begin a job expecting the company to design a success plan for them, if they are good workers; or expecting the right time to come along for them to begin college for a real career.

During this waiting process, however, a bell doesn't ring to announce the right place and the right time to begin a real career success plan. One day on the job turns into another day on the job - another week - another month - another year. A great wave of sudden emotion and inspiration doesn't suddenly appear to announce, "Now is the time to start a firm success plan for yourself." Lifestyle demands of food, shelter, clothing, increasing costs, and other financial demands push the concept of beginning a personal self-development program further into the abyss of a vague and distant dream.

The absence of a clear plan for a more successful future, with the anticipation of being more in control of one's decisions about his or her future, is the basis for worker alienation. A worker's resignation to the reality that he or she will always be told what to do at a common job creates an antithesis of that position. The worker must have that job to survive; but the worker understands that the job will never permit him or her to have any control to make a valuable contribution. The worker becomes alienated from that situation.

Under the control of alienation a worker cannot fully focus on the demands, the seriousness, and the importance of his or her unimportant job. Since that worker cannot become job-focused, when the situation demands job-focus, conflict naturally results.

Worker alienation is ordinarily blamed on workplace conditions, poor management and leadership, lack of good motivational techniques, and poor job design. New management concepts are even designed to overcome this natural condition of alienation in the workplace. These desperate experimental concepts include: quality circles, worker empowerment, team management, work enlargement, and total quality management programs.

Although these experimental concepts offer workers a temporary source to fulfill the belonging, ego and esteem needs, described by Abraham Maslow, these concepts offer nothing to fulfill that highest need of self-actualization. Regardless of the type of experimental management concept used, those workers' lives are still controlled by the management environment. They remain alienated from being in control of their own destiny. Once the distraction and newness of these experimental programs vanish, conflict and alienation will certainly reestablish themselves.

To decrease the feeling and condition of alienation by workers, workers must believe that they are in control of their lives and their destiny. This process cannot be accomplished by management style or management technique. It must be developed by the worker who understands the personal success planning process. Most workers don't understand this process for they've never been exposed to it.

If managers want to eliminate the conflict that accompanies alienation and restricts productivity in the average workplace they must teach this process to their workers. This simple but important process will be explained in the chapter titled, *Employeeship* Considerations. An example will be given here, however, to demonstrate how the absence of a proactive success plan allows workers to develop a feeling of alienation.

An example: Don's dilemma

Don Matthews was a recent high school graduate when he entered the workforce. He was anxious to begin a career, to make enough money to buy a new car and to afford marriage and a place of his own; hopefully a nice pad. He found a good job the week before he graduated from high school and began work two weeks after he graduated. He deserved a two-week vacation before going to work.

He began his job as a packager at the local apparel manufacturing company, Foremost Fashions. His job was to sort finished products: shirts, blouses, sleep wear and children's clothing, into packages and cartons for shipping to retail outlets. He was comfortable with his job, and within the next two weeks considered himself fully qualified; an expert. His pay at this time was a dollar above minimum wage, which he considered sufficient to provide all the things that he needed at the time, since he stilled lived at home with his parents.

Don constantly was rushed at his job, since he was the only

packager. He had learned so quickly and was so proficient that the other packager, who was there when Don arrived, was moved to another section with an increase in pay. This was encouraging for Don for he felt that his abilities would quickly be recognized, and he would be moved up to a higher status job that would include a higher pay scale. Although he really didn't need the extra money now, any promotion would be something that he could show off.

No one bothered Don during his first six months on the job. In fact, he rarely saw the senior manager of the plant and he talked with his immediate supervisor only once or twice a day. He hoped his supervisor liked him and appreciated his work, but he wasn't sure. His supervisor never asked Don for an opinion, but fortunately his supervisor never complained about his performance, either. At the end of that six months Don felt that he was doing his job the best that it could be done and that this performance would be recognized during his six-month review by his supervisor.

The week after the end of Don's first six months on the job Don's supervisor asked Don to come into his office for a talk. The supervisor asked Don to sit in a chair and to be comfortable. He also asked Don if he would like a cup of coffee. The supervisor followed the 'book' on preparing a subordinate for a counseling session. Don felt comfortable in the supervisor's office, not only from the fact that he knew that he would be recognized for doing a wonderful job, but also from the confidence that he had from being a high school graduate who had found a job immediately upon graduation.

The supervisor began the performance review by telling Don how much all the people in the plant, including himself, enjoyed Don's attitude and performance. His comments were that Don was "a good guy to work with and a motivated person who never backed away from hard work." He also reinforced this statement with the comment that Don had learned his job faster than anyone else before him. Don was very pleased with himself.

Don noticed that the supervisor had been gingerly fingering a standard manila folder on his desk while he was talking to Don.

After the initial statement of how well Don was appreciated and respected by his peers and by management, the supervisor slid a form from inside that manila folder. Don could tell immediately that the form was not a standard letter; it had blocks, squares and lines on it to segment different types of information.

While looking over that form, the supervisor told Don that it was time for his six-month's performance review. He told Don, "We want to make sure that everyone who works here understands his or her weak points and strong points so they can make improvements on the weak points and keep up the good work on the strong points." The supervisor asked Don to slide his chair closer to his desk so that he could explain each of the rating factors; the form remained on the supervisor's desk.

There were eight individual rating factors on the evaluation form that included work characteristics and personality characteristics. Each of those factors had a rating range of from one to ten. Don's ratings in those factors were from six to eight. His overall rating was a seven. This was the rating designated as very good.

Don asked the supervisor to explain what was necessary for him to be rated in the higher overall ratings of excellent, outstanding, and superior. The supervisor answered that these ratings were usually reserved for people with more experience, and who were able to make a bigger contribution to the organization. He consoled Don that if he kept up his good work and his good attitude that he would probably be rated higher as time went along. The supervisor told Don that for his first evaluation it's better to leave room to "show growth." Don was asked to sign the form to acknowledge that he had read it, understood it, and had discussed it with his supervisor.

Don left his supervisor's office with a feeling of trapped despair. He knew that he had done at least outstanding work since he had been at his new job. He had even replaced two ordinary workers; yet, since he was new, he wasn't eligible for a higher rating to recognize his effort. Don also knew that he would probably never be moved from that job since he did it so well. Advancement, recognition, and more opportunities were probably out of reach for him in the immediate future. Although Don didn't openly complain about his evaluation rating, he felt hurt, isolated, and helpless. What could he do? Nothing!

Later that day, during a fifteen-minute break, Don asked a group of his friends about the ratings in that office. He asked, "Are high ratings ever given" and "Who usually gets the higher ratings?" Most of the workers who had been there over two years knew everything about those ratings and evaluations. They had heard all the promises and the rationalizations as they were counseled during the evaluation process. They had also learned from clerks in the personnel department that the plant manager allowed only twenty percent of the appraisals to be above the 'very good' level; and even those required an additional page of written justification.

Don felt even more trapped, for he knew that a system rather than his direct supervisor determined his level of formal recognition for his personal efforts. Since he was new, he also felt he wouldn't be rated higher than 'very good' for a long time, regardless of his level of work.

In effect, the system was designed to be discouraging rather than fair and motivational. Don decided to agree with the other workers in his area: "It's just not worth busting your butt if the company doesn't care about you."

This example of Don demonstrates the typical beginning of the process of alienation in the workplace. Furthermore, all four dimensions of alienation discussed above are active in Don's story. Top management requires archaic appraisal reports, for they assume by historical acceptance that detailed appraisal reports are necessary. Middle managers, even if they know of the demotivational effects of oppressive systems, will not compromise themselves by trying to buck the "system." Supervisors really have no choice; they must do what they are told and enforce oppressive policies face-to-face with workers.

This face-to-face contact is normally the only place where conflict becomes open and obvious. When this happens, workers usually realize their companies will not be fair and operate with any of their concerns as part of the company interest. This realization that they are considered only tools causes many workers to de-personalize themselves. De-personalization against an unfair process is the catalyst for alienation.

The nature of many jobs doesn't always permit workers to be appropriately recognized, or to allow them any anticipation of meaningful work and advancement. Some jobs, on the other hand, do possess these characteristics, but they are often disregarded by oppressive or unknowledgeable leaders. In either case, a worker who feels that leaders are interested only in productivity and their own esteem needs will become alienated and a source of conflict, unless that worker has a plan for personal self-fulfillment.

Workers ordinarily aren't trained that success is a continuing self-developmental process. It's not necessarily achieved only at the present job or at any one job. Leaders must teach this success process to those workers who cannot find an alternative to conflict and alienation by themselves. If not, productivity will continue to be influenced by the level of conflict. This success process is explained in the chapter on Employeeship.

Summary

Although workplace conflict is the fundamental cause of most inefficiency and productivity weaknesses in most organizations, those that don't function at a hundred percent of their optimum capability, that workplace conflict is the last factor to be recognized as the real problem. Problems are quickly attributed to other conditions such as: lazy or untrained workers, late delivery times of parts and supplies, weak supervisors, lack of effective communications, and general malaise and demotivation in the organization. The condition of workplace conflict is rarely, if ever, acknowledged as the primary source of weak productivity.

Workplace conflict is ignored as the cause of organizational problems because the people, leaders, who identify organizational problems would be pointing the 'blame finger' at themselves if they were to admit conflict existed in the workplace to a level that would jeopardize productivity.

It's easier and safer to blame other factors that have no self-defensive mechanisms. Efforts to resolve productivity problems by focusing on other more popular causes rarely result in fundamental and lasting improvement. Temporary solutions are found in one area until the fundamental problem rears its ugly head in another area. Then the problem must be solved again in that new area. Until the fundamental problem of workplace conflict is acknowledged as the core problem in most workplaces, the fundamental antithesis to natural workplace productivity will most probably never be eliminated. In other words, it must be recognized and acknowledged as a problem for that problem to be solved.

Workplace conflict and disharmony may be generated and exist at any level of an organization. Furthermore, that conflict doesn't remain at the level at which it's generated. Conflict that develops at any level will affect efficiency, cooperation, and productivity at all other levels. Each level of potential conflict should be identified as a conflict dimension, for it's an area that may be evaluated individually but has universal effects on the total organization.

Although conflict may exist at any level of an organization and it may be generated at any level of an organization, the negative influence that it exhibits occurs most significantly at the working level of the organization. That's usually the level between the supervisor and the worker. These are the two levels in an organization where goals, cultures and values clash. Supervisors are responsible for productivity; and workers who are alienated attempt to defend their rights to be treated as people, not merely as unintelligent tools used for that productivity.

The remaining chapters of this book are designed to eliminate the conflict zone to encourage natural productivity. Ideas are presented for leaders to use to show their workers that those workers really are important. A success plan is also explained to encourage workers to find self-fulfillment, regardless of the quality of leadership in their work environments.

2

CONFLICT SOURCES

Conflict in an organization doesn't just happen. Someone does something or fails to do something that causes or generates that conflict. Conflict has been recognized as a major contributor to workplace inefficiency and disharmony since management and employee relationships began, particularly since the early 1900s. Most management attempts to reduce workplace conflict have focused on trying to improve communications in the workplace. Most of those attempts have failed.

Those attempts have failed for two fundamental reasons. First, that emphasis traditionally has been focused on the symptoms of conflict, not on the cause of conflict itself. Secondly, many leaders perceive morale as synonymous with cooperation, motivation, and workplace harmony.

Management often becomes focused on those symptoms and the outward reactions of conflict. Conflict exists at some level in all organizations but it doesn't appear as hostility, defiance, reluctance, and lack of cooperation until it grows large enough to become visible. Until that happens, it's assumed there's no conflict in the organization.

Conflict silently creeps as withheld productivity, malaise, tardiness, and high worker turnover. Since management is usually preoccupied: trying to improve productivity with new procedures and incentives; trying to increase motivation to eliminate the malaise in the organization; trying to increase disciplinary measures to eliminate

27

the tardiness problem, and trying to improve morale to decrease the high worker turnover rate, management doesn't have time or the inclination to resolve the fundamental conflict problem. Management is usually trying to hit an unseen target with a scatter gun. Most organizations fail to hit the target. The fundamental problem, conflict, remains under the surface, unseen.

The Conflict Definition

An understanding of the concept of workplace conflict is necessary before further analysis may have real meaning. Conflict in the workplace is the natural condition, not the exception; however, open hostility that signals the existence of conflict may be the exception. It's socially acceptable to have feelings of conflict, dislike, distrust, and antagonism; but to openly display those feelings isn't ordinarily considered an act of a rational and socially trained person. These emotional feelings usually must be extreme to become visible.

Workplace conflict occurs on two levels. One level is that which ordinarily is considered as workplace conflict. This occurs when differences of opinion result in loud arguments, threats, and intimidation from any member of that work environment. This is personality based conflict.

The second level is that which occurs from worker actions and reactions that affect productivity and efficiency, but doesn't necessarily include differences in personality. This is system based conflict. Personality based conflict usually gets most of the attention and emphasis toward correction. System based conflict usually goes unobserved and creates most of the productivity damage.

Sources of Conflict

There are two basic sources of workplace conflict. These two

28

sources are leaders and workers. Simply, leaders create conflict by using too much leadership or too little leadership; and workers cause conflict by their acquiescence of good employeeship, which includes focusing on a personal success plan. Although conflict shows itself by other means, these are the two fundamental sources. These will be analyzed individually:

Leadership created Conflict

Although workplace conflict ordinarily is attributed to lack of ability, understanding, concern, and malaise of workers, according to leaders; much of that conflict is initiated, encouraged, or allowed by those leaders. Although workers may realize leaders are responsible for much of the conflict in a workplace, those workers usually have no forum to make their beliefs credible. They may express that leaders are responsible for much of the conflict, but there's no one who listens to their comments. Even if someone were to listen to workers' complaints, those listeners ordinarily would have no authority to make corrective changes.

Leaders may cause workplace conflict, often identified as disharmony, through many ordinary influences. The most important of these include:

1. The leader's personality

2. The leader's basic values

3. The leader's training and background

4. The leader's management style

5. The leader's frustration tolerance

6. Pressure on the leader from above

7. Desire for an alternative situation

These influences will be discussed, individually:

Personality

The leader's personality is a major factor often ignored as a basis of harmony and productivity. An individual's personality is considered an important part of that person in worldly affairs, except when that person enters into a work environment. Then it's ordinarily assumed the workplace takes on an impersonal characteristic; where only facts, policies, and procedures demand any consideration. Personality isn't considered as a workplace factor.

A leader's basic charter is ordinarily to treat subordinates dispassionately but equitably. It's assumed that all decisions and actions should be made on the basis of logic and merit, not on the basis of personality considerations. Many business hierarchal structures contain an unwritten code that leaders shouldn't exhibit their normal personalities to their subordinates, for it might make them appear mortal, and vulnerable to control and manipulation by greedy and lazy subordinates. The remainder of the world outside the workplace places high regard on personality in persuading others to reach goals.

Basic Values

Persons in leadership positions and lower-level worker positions have basic value differences. Basically, the leader feels he or she must do whatever is necessary to accomplish his or her goals of productivity and performance. Workers, except those rare and extraordinary ones, tend to feel they should do no more than they are paid to do. And since, in most cases, workers tend to feel they aren't paid as much as they're worth, they aren't inclined to do everything required simply to reach company goals.

Leaders' basic workplace values are focused on efficiency and productivity. Workers' basic workplace values are related to fairness. This antithesis of values is not only a source of basic conflict, it's also the concept that gives credibility and influence to labor organizations.

Training Background

Leaders receive different types and levels of management training. Some learn on-the-job, while others learn management and leadership concepts in a more formal education environment. Those who learn through experience tend to have ideas and opinions that reflect fixed and unchangeable ideas toward productivity. "Since it's always been done this way," that must be the right way to do it; and in most cases those opinions are focused only on the job and not on employee concerns.

On the other hand, many leaders are trained in a more formal environment that emphasizes scientific management principles and process engineering. This training also tends to disregard the concern for employee motivations and feelings. In either case, a leader who cannot or does not consider worker concerns in the productivity process will create conflict in the organization.

Management Style

Some leaders create conflict and alienation in an organization by their leadership style. An autocratic leader assumes workers are no good, lazy, and must be driven to become productive. This leadership philosophy is taken from a management style explained by Douglas McGregor as the Theory X approach of management.

The opposite style of management known as human relations, democratic, or behavioral management also includes some conflict, even with the highest intentions by management to eliminate that conflict. The basis for this management style is the leadership approach identified by Douglas McGregor as the Theory Y leadership approach. This approach assumes workers are inwardly motivated and desire to seek achievement and meaningful work. Some workers anticipate and expect a more autocratic approach by management, and when that style isn't used those workers develop the resentment of not having a strong leader, again inducing conflict into the organization.

Frustration Levels

Some leaders have lower levels of frustration tolerance than do others. Even leaders with high levels of worker concerns at times lose their ability to remain in emotional control to show that concern. This situation is more applicable to human relations leaders than to more autocratic leaders, since autocratic leaders have established no history of worker concerns. Their lack of worker concern and usually their high level of anticipation, control, and frustration routinely have been established. A high state of conflict routinely exists in the workplace led by an autocratic leader. Some workers become desensitized to that environment, or if they have always worked in that environment they might think that condition is only normal.

Human relations leaders, those who care about the needs of workers, ordinarily are in more real control of their environments. They delegate authority to let their subordinates share some responsibility for accomplishing their tasks. To maintain a high level of harmony and productivity, however, these leaders must understand the emotional and esteem needs of their workers. They do this by observing changes in emotional moods of their subordinates. A leader who becomes frustrated with job conditions or personal problems will often forget the necessity to maintain a stable environment. In that situation, the normal reaction is for the leader to revert to a more insensitive and autocratic leadership style, unless that leader is confident and experienced.

Pressure from Superiors

Many lower level leaders who are directly responsible for worker productivity aren't allowed to be leaders on their own terms and by their own authority. There are many senior leaders in the business and industrial world who will not, or cannot, effectively delegate real authority to their subordinate leaders. The organizational chart might appear to separate that function, and the senior leader might really think he or she has delegated that authority; but even with this assumed delineation, delegation doesn't really exist. The senior leader must check, make sure, assist, suggest, and help that subordinate leader with those details. Most often, these actions are nothing more than interference that creates conflict and undermines any positive influence of the subordinate leader.

Unnecessary interference or pressure by senior leaders creates compound conflict rather than simple conflict in an organization. Although the conflict between the two levels of leadership might not be open and obvious, nevertheless, it exists. Workers, on the other hand, may respond in various ways that are more open and obvious. Some workers will show resentment toward the subordinate leader for not "standing up for his or her rights." Some workers will try to bypass the authority and control of the subordinate leader to gain more personal influence and control. Some workers will show sympathy toward the subordinate leader for not being allowed to do his or her job. Other workers will assume this is another normal symptom of the "screwed up" organization. And, others will exhibit normal defensive reactions to frustration, such as withdrawal or aggression.

Regardless of the response, the reaction or the emotional feelings of those workers, productive harmony will not exist in that organization. Conflict and disharmony reign in those organizations that don't allow harmonious conditions to be developed and maintained. Pressure and unnecessary interference with the direct relationships between first-line leaders and workers are major causes of serious conflict in many organizations.

Ordinarily, the negative condition becomes worse, which invites more direct control by the senior leader. Eventually the cause of declining productivity is identified, by the senior leader, as weak and demotivated workers or incompetent first-line leaders. The topic of delegation will be analyzed further in the chapter titled, Leadership Forces.

Desire for Alternatives

Many motivated and otherwise competent leaders are in the wrong career. They feel trapped in their jobs and desire alternatives that may offer more emotional rewards and job satisfaction. In the right job environment they might be outstanding leaders and motivators, but in a non-homogeneous job they become a source of demotivation which may easily evolve into workplace conflict.

Most workers prefer their leaders to be interested, enthusiastic and dedicated. These leadership qualities give workers a feeling of direction, security, and purpose, and enhance their opportunities for achievement and recognition. Workers realize their reputations, their chance for esteem, and status, can be no greater in the organization than that of their leader's. Since achievement and recognition are two of the important motivators, workers tend to become frustrated or demotivated if the reasonable possibility to achieve these conditions doesn't exist. This frustration ordinarily evolves into conflict.

Following is an example to demonstrate how leaders often initiate workplace conflict that they interpret as being caused by workers. This example concerns an event between Martin C. and his supervisor in a corrugated container manufacturing plant::

Martin was a general handy man in the plant. His job was to insure raw corrugated sheets were stocked at each of the processing forms so boxes could continue to be made without interruption by other workers who were experienced with forming machines. Martin was also responsible for general housekeeping and cleanliness in the plant.

Although this was a low-status job in that plant, it was the best job Martin ever had. His prior work experience had been as a general laborer through a temporary employment agency. Those jobs were usually daily assignment situations that included dirty and tiresome work.

Martin's supervisor, Ed, reminded Martin every day of the importance of keeping each location sufficiently stocked with raw cardboard to insure the form processing could continue to operate without interruptions. Ed reiterated to Martin the resupply function was more important than housekeeping and the appearance of the plant, except for those housekeeping functions that concerned safety matters. Martin made this the top priority in his list of assignments, because he knew how important this was to Ed. He never failed to have an adequate supply of raw cardboard on hand at each location.

After a period of several weeks, he was beginning to become annoyed with the constant reminder by Ed that sufficient stocks should be maintained at each location. He began to feel Ed didn't like him or didn't trust him, otherwise, Ed would recognize that he knew how to do his job. The constant reminder became a form of harassment, even when Martin would respond with stronger emphasis that he was aware of that important requirement. Eventually, Ed accused Martin of having an attitude problem.

One day Ed's manager called Ed into his office and suggested to Ed that his area of the plant looked like a garbage dump most of the time. Ed and his manager got along fairly well, but Ed wasn't comfortable enough with their relationship to risk taking the blame for the appearance in the plant. Ed told his manager that he has told them and told them to keep the place neat but, "you know how those useless workers are; they just don't listen now-a-days." Ed assured his manager that he would straighten his workers out right away.

Ed went directly to Martin and told Martin, "You really got me into hot water with my boss. He just chewed me out for the appearance of this place. You know you are responsible for keeping this place clean."

Martin didn't know what to say. He knew if he gave the logical response, that he was following the established priority of his tasks, that he would again be accused of having an attitude problem. If he asked for more help, he felt he might be accused of being lazy. He told Ed he would try to keep the place cleaner, even if he had to work through his break periods sometimes. Ed replied, "Just so the boss doesn't get on my hide again."

Martin worked faster to avoid another confrontation. He felt the situation was unfair, because Ed had not stood up for him and the manager didn't trust Ed enough to ask his opinion or to respect his suggestions. Martin had no logical way out; he was really exploited by management. Martin knew even if he quit his job it would be difficult to find another permanent job. He would most likely even need a recommendation from his current manager to be accepted into another job. He also knew his manager thought he was lazy and incompetent because his supervisor had reinforced that impression.

In his desperation and alienation, however, Martin did find an escape from his dilemma. He learned of the worker's compensation, injury, and anxious lawyer litigation process. Within two weeks, Martin had a severe back injury, which no one witnessed, and within six months he had a settlement check for $22,000.

One might suggest this situation couldn't happen, that it's only theoretical. Those who are exposed to the business and industrial work environment know many workers file false worker's claims for reasons much less serious than those of alienation and conflict. Some do it for it's an easy way to get quick and easy money. Some do it in response to enticement by aggressive attorney pressure advertising.

Many do it as a way to escape from the conflict created and perpetuated by their leaders. For some, it's the only logical modern alternative.

This example is a clear demonstration that leaders cause much of the conflict in work environments. This example also demonstrates how workers are almost always blamed as the source of that conflict. The only people who could effectively blame leaders as sources of conflict are themselves, and they aren't likely to do that.

This brief analysis of some major causes of leader-initiated workplace conflict is not only to show those major causes, but also to emphasize that much workplace conflict that's attributed to lazy workers and weak first-line management might have higher management as its real source. During an organizational analysis of weak productivity, organizational disharmony, and open and aggressive conflict, senior leaders in the organization should resist the temptation to disregard their own actions as a fundamental source of that conflict.

Since the purpose of an organization's productivity analysis is to improve productivity, real problems and real solutions should be considered not merely those that are convenient and safe. Ignoring or refusing to see real problems is the source of greater tragedies for an organization. Problems, not symptoms of problems, should be solved.

Another important differentiation should be made at this time regarding conflict, harmony, and morale. High morale is an important attribute in an organization, but high morale shouldn't be considered synonymous with workplace harmony and absence of conflict.

Workplace morale refers to the compatibility of personalities and to the focus in an organization to eliminate disagreements and different avenues of expression. High morale suggests happiness and compatibility. Happiness and compatibility don't necessarily create productivity, which is the fundamental purpose of an organization. An organization has a bonus if it has good morale along with high productivity, but high morale doesn't create that high productivity.

High productivity is permitted in an organization by

harmonious working relationships. These harmonious relationships may exist only when the level of workplace conflict is reduced to its optimum level. Workplace conflict doesn't refer to conflict of attitudes or conflict of personalities. A leader who makes the assumption it does is soon focusing on trying to improve morale, instead of trying to eliminate workplace conflict. Workplace conflict refers to the response initiated by workers, or induced by leaders, that results in withheld productivity by workers. It's possible maximum productivity may exist in an organization that's characterized by low levels of morale. Maximum productivity most likely cannot be maintained in an organization that's ruled by conflicting purposes.

Worker-initiated Conflict

Leadership actions aren't the only sources of conflict in a typical work environment. Workers must also share the responsibility for much conflict that results in low performance and productivity. Low productivity not only harms effectiveness of an organization, which may be one aim of that reduced productivity, it also creates harm to those workers who choose to withhold productivity. While attempting to damage a leader or an organization that's perceived to be exploitive and unfair, workers ultimately do more damage to themselves by that intentional conflict.

Conflict initiated by workers also has several causes. Some are intentional and some are caused by a lack of focus on tasks and responsibilities. The following causes of worker-initiated conflict will be discussed here, briefly, only for acknowledgment. They will be discussed in more detail in the chapter titled, Goals of Harmony. These causes include:

1. Laziness

2. Demotivation

3. Cultural Conflict

4. Lack of Goals - Frustration

5. Time Alternatives

These will be described briefly to demonstrate their relationships to workplace conflict:

Laziness

In his book, *Possibility Thinking*, Robert Schuller writes, "The temptation to laziness never grows old." This concept applies to the workplace as well as to any other place in society. Normally when productivity goals aren't achieved, laziness is often blamed regardless of the real cause of that inefficiency.

It takes a special person to avoid the temptation to laziness. Even the best and most productive workers cannot be expected to work at full speed at all times. Unfortunately, once they set their habits and productivity levels, any reduction or decrease in those established levels of productivity may be interpreted by their leaders as a sign of laziness.

Whether the condition of laziness is determined by fact or by comparing work habits of workers who vary their work pace, leaders are, nevertheless, on guard to make immediate correction to those workers who exhibit any sign of laziness. Any attempt by leaders, whether valid or invalid, to reduce worker laziness increases the conflict potential in an organization. The elimination of laziness is one of management's primary functions for existing as leaders.

Demotivation

Conflict is often caused by worker demotivation. Many

naturally motivated workers may eventually become demotivated. This demotivation might result from a worker's inner thoughts and perceptions about himself or herself and the job, which is internal demotivation; or it might occur in response to an influence outside the worker's thoughts. This demotivation might be the reaction from an event or a condition in the workplace or in one's personal affairs. This demotivation would be identified as external demotivation. Ordinarily, demotivation would have a stronger negative influence than would any attempts to motivate that person by more positive motivational techniques.

Regardless of its source or its cause, demotivation is still demotivation. It would be reflected in the attitude or the job performance of a worker who had been demotivated. A bad attitude or weaker job performance would, again, create a situation to create conflict in the organization. The characteristics of demotivation are explained more fully in the chapter titled, Goals of Harmony.

Peer Pressure

Many potentially dedicated and loyal workers often aren't allowed to be good, dedicated, and loyal workers by other workers who are less motivated to help the organization reach its goals. The forceful power some workers have over others is that force, usually a negative force, identified as peer pressure. Peer pressure in a workplace is normally a negative influence; and it exists in any workplace. That negative influence is so strong in many organizations that potential super-stars aren't allowed to be even significant workers.

Peer pressure creates two significant areas of conflict, as well as frustration. Conflict is created when leaders must take direct action to encourage workers to improve their productivity. Workers ordinarily resent this effort by management, even when it's warranted and necessary, and even when workers intentionally withhold productivity. Conflict is also created within a potential super-star's self-image, for that person becomes frustrated by conflicting goals and drives. Frustration is ordinarily interpreted as normal conflict, as well as disinterest in productivity.

Cultural Influence

A worker's cultural background and history often determine and influence that worker's attitude toward the workplace and toward leaders in the workplace. A worker from a culturally deprived environment will ordinarily approach the work environment with different expectations than will a leader or a worker from a broader background. Workers from lower cultures ordinarily anticipate less success and less return on their personal effort. In general they cannot understand a rational reason for making a direct contribution to their work environment.

With this negative, and less inspired expectation of fair treatment and an equal chance to become "somebody" in life, many of these culturally deprived workers don't feel the real motivation to exert themselves. As a result, their motivational needs remain obscured by an attitude of despair and skepticism. Because they ordinarily don't anticipate success and fair treatment, it's unusual when leaders can provide those things that permit harmony and the avoidance of conflict in a work environment.

Lack of Clear Goals

Many workers remain frustrated and ambivalent in the workplace; not because they don't receive what they want, but because they are too frustrated to know what they want. They haven't determined what they really want from life generally, and what they want from the workplace, specifically. These workers wait for leaders in the workplace to assign those goals for them and to make the achievement of those goals easy and automatic. This condition is created when workers refuse, or don't know how, to design a personal success plan.

Two points of conflict occur when workers fail to have a success plan. First, they must assume leaders are responsible for their careers and the level of their success. When this doesn't happen, when leaders continue to emphasize productivity and the individual's personal responsibility for himself or herself, workers often imagine those leaders are barriers "holding them back" from more money, more prestige, and more success. This conflict in perceptions is perhaps the major source for the concept of worker exploitation in management-worker relations.

The second point of conflict, when a worker fails to have a personal success plan, is that of frustration. Workers, as well as other people, tend to become frustrated when they cannot achieve important goals, even when they don't know what those goals are. These personal frustrations appear as defensive mechanisms which contain built-in conflict.

As an example, one of those defensive mechanisms is identified as projection. In this case, the worker would project another's feelings and thoughts as his or her own. The most popular form and use of projection in the work environment is the statement, "I can't get ahead because my supervisor hates me." Under this logic, if a person has no success plan or goals, that person cannot blame himself or herself for failing to achieve those goals. It's "somebody else's fault." Conflict is an inherent part of work environment relationships where each member of that environment places blame for failure on another person.

Alternative Use of Time

Even a worker who is career-oriented and who loves his or her job would rather be somewhere else doing something else, at least occasionally. There are other pleasant alternatives to work even when one enjoys work. There are grand-daddy fish waiting to be caught. There are golf courses that need someone to create new grass growth by digging deep divots. There are tennis courts that need someone to serve zinging aces. There are lonely relatives who need someone to visit them. And, there are places that need to be seen simply for their natural beauty: New England in autumn, Florida beaches, California forests, the Grand Canyon and the Painted Desert. Even many dedicated workers feel they should be in a college or a university to improve their educational levels for continuing self-development.

Less career-oriented workers have other alternatives that are as important. These alternatives include more sleep, hanging-out, and being a couch potato with enough beer and snacks to last all day.

Regardless of one's interests, there's usually something many would prefer to do rather than remain at the job all day, everyday, every week, every month. When these interests rise above the normal level; when they become dominating desires, they usually create actions that result in some level of conflict. That conflict might be latent or at a low level, but it's there to influence work environment relationships.

Let's examine an event that demonstrates how some workers, regardless of management's concern for them, will be a natural source of workplace conflict. This example concerns Hazel in the administrative department of a trucking company:

Hazel had been at her job with the trucking company for about six months. During her first five months on the job, Hazel had been interested in her job. She was still learning and she had been courteous and cooperative with her peers as well as with her supervisor and manager. During the sixth month, however, Hazel's attitude toward the workplace and toward people in the workplace began to change.

She became less patient with her co-workers, she began to debate minor points with her supervisor, and nothing seemed to satisfy her personality. According to Hazel, her co-workers were lazy and stupid, the room was too warm or too cold, and her supervisor should "stay out of her face." Obviously, she wasn't a happy or satisfied person. Eventually, she became so uncooperative that her supervisor, Gladys, decided to counsel Hazel about her human relations skills.

When Hazel met with Gladys in a private area Gladys went through all the steps suggested to insure an effective counseling session. This included casual conversation to help Hazel relax, and compliments on the positive aspects of Hazel's job performance. In about five minutes, Gladys felt the condition was right to discuss the major point of Hazel's performance that needed to be improved.

To open the serious conversation Gladys said, "Hazel, although your ability shows potential for the future, demonstrated by your early performance, your work habits at this time are causing some problems for yourself as well as others working around you. We need to discuss that situation to see if you can determine a more successful course for yourself. Have you noticed, lately, that your attitude and your performance haven't been as positive as they were when you began work here?"

Hazel replied, "I do my job and that's what I get paid for isn't it?" Gladys was glad Hazel answered her question with a question, for it gave her an opportunity to move into the counseling phase, naturally, without being the initiator of ideas.

Gladys explained to Hazel that, "Your job is to be a positive part of the organization; not only to work at your direct productivity process, but to help make conditions favorable so that others, including myself, can do their jobs in harmony. You get paid to be a contributing member of the total organization. That's your real job."

Hazel's response to that comment gave the clue to the source of her attitude and actions; "Well, it seems to me that the more I work here, the harder I try, the less appreciation I get for what I do. No one really appreciates what I do, and no one wants to help me get ahead."

Gladys asked, "Oh, what are you trying to do to improve your future that the company might help you with? As you might not be aware, the company encourages its people to improve themselves with education and other self-development efforts."

The direct cause of her conflict exposed itself with Hazel's answer. "I have been working here for a long time now, and neither you or anybody else has helped me get ahead. It seems that I will be stuck at this job forever. When I came into the company I wanted to be able to do something for myself."

Gladys asked, "What have you done to improve yourself for those opportunities? Are you taking some courses? Are you going to college in the evening?"

Hazel answered, "No, but I've been doing my job the best I can, and I've been thinking about starting some college courses."

Gladys pressed Hazel further with another timely question, "What college courses do you plan to take, and what do you plan to do in the future to really advance yourself?" Hazel replied that she didn't "really know."

Gladys felt that this was a good time, and a good place, to conclude the counseling session. She complimented Hazel on her decision to begin her educational improvement, and she offered to help with course selection and some study time if that became essential and critical. She also encouraged Hazel to determine what she really wanted to do in the future, by determining some definite goals.

Of course she was careful to insure that Hazel felt that those suggestions were Hazel's ideas and conclusions. She closed with a reminder that work habits and attitude in the workplace were important parts of career development.

This example demonstrates that workers often tend to cause problems, conflict, for themselves and often jeopardize their careers by not having definite goals planned for a career. Many workers assume management is responsible for planning and managing their careers. This assumption causes conflict, for when management doesn't perform that function anticipated by workers those workers assume management is "holding us back from advancement."

This feeling by workers directly attacks their self-esteem, which is one of the important motivators. Their reactions to that frustration is usually one of the defensive reactions to frustration.

Summary

Conflict is a symptom and a reaction to many other forces and influences that affect the character, the quality, and the effectiveness of a work environment. Workplace conflict has existed for such a long time that it's become accepted as a natural member of normal working conditions.

Workplace conflict isn't a natural or an automatic event that must occur. It has specific causes and sources clearly identifiable. There are only two fundamental sources of conflict, which are leaders and workers.

Perceptions and self-interests ordinarily force leaders to blame workers for workplace conflict. Many leaders who adopt the Theory X management approach assume workers are naturally unconcerned and lazy. This perception creates a natural conflict base.

Perceptions and self-interests also force many workers to blame leaders for workplace conflict that's not necessarily caused by leaders. Although there are many leaders who follow the Theory X principle of leadership, there are also at least as many leaders who try to improve the quality of life for workers; while at the same time, maintain an effective level of productivity in the organization. Workers who cannot or do not respond to these positive attempts by leaders ordinarily have no success plan for themselves. Furthermore, they're defeated by low self-esteem, they have narrow ranges of personality, or they believe that they cannot succeed in life - and they intend to prove it.

Workplace conflict can be reduced, especially in most large

and complex work environments, which could increase productivity as much as ten to twenty percent. One source estimates the average worker produces at about fifty percent of his or her capability. Conflict may even be eliminated in many of the more simple work environments that have a socially and culturally compatible workforce, and leaders who follow the concepts of Theory Y leadership.

Managing The Conflict Zone

3

LEADERSHIP FORCES

To a large degree leadership is like the weather. Everybody discusses it, everybody's concerned about it; but rarely does anybody seriously attempt to do anything about it. Weather has a flow pattern that can only be discussed, not changed. Leadership also has a pattern; it's always being discussed about planning for improvement - *someday.*

From a practical view, most business and industrial organizations have management philosophies that tend to perpetuate themselves, regardless of any attempt to change. Organizational leadership exists for self-survival. Change, even for improvement, threatens that level of security.

The purpose for this chapter is briefly to analyze various factors and influences that affect the quality and results of leaders' efforts in work environments that directly or indirectly influence conflict in those environments. The purpose is not to thoroughly analyze each of those individual factors, for there are many other sources readily available to accomplish that purpose. This chapter is not intended to repeat that standard information, but to synthesize many of those leadership factors. This synthesis is important to help understand the basics of leadership styles, factors, and influences that contribute to disharmony and conflict in many work environments.

49

Leadership Styles

There are three basic leadership styles. These are the autocratic style, the democratic style, and the non-leader style. Although there are other names or labels for these different styles, these names include those same meanings. For those new students or new practitioners, these styles will be briefly defined:

The Autocratic Leadership Style

The autocratic leader, also known as the authoritarian leader, is one who disregards the higher needs of his or her subordinates. Basic needs such as job security and level of pay might not be affected by the actions of an autocratic leader, for an autocratic leader might exist in an environment of high pay and job benefits. The autocratic leader doesn't permit subordinates to reach those higher needs of self-esteem, achievement, and recognition; and is ordinarily recognized from the following traits:

- A leader who acts as though he or she is more intelligent than everyone else

- A leader who cannot or will not delegate authority to fulfill a subordinate's responsibility

- A leader who's insensitive to subordinates' feelings and needs

- A leader who trusts no one, and must be in charge of everything

- A leader who claims full credit for progress, but shifts blame to someone else for any mistakes

- A leader who considers only engineering processes in the workplace

- A leader who has no long range plans.

The autocratic leader functions from a power base of position authority, fear, impatience, and intimidation. This leader must receive all the applause, and is resentful of subordinates who become personally recognized for their individual efforts. The autocratic leader acts as if he or she is the only person in the organization who knows what must be done, when it must be done, and how it should be done. Workers are in the workplace only to do what they are instructed to do. The work environment managed by an autocratic leader normally exhibits the following characteristics:

An atmosphere of fear and apprehension

Bickering among workers

Fault-finding among workers

Job disharmony

Constantly recurring problems

An "I just work here" attitude

Reluctance to make even minor decisions

Major fluctuations of productivity

No training for key growth positions

From a practical viewpoint of the leadership definition, an autocratic leader is not a leader. An autocratic leader is a director of action who merely uses people to do those things he or she directs. Directing is only one of the five essential functions of management.

The other leadership functions are: *planning, organizing, coordinating* and *controlling.*

The Democratic Leadership Style

The democratic style is also known as the human relations style. The democratic leader is concerned with efficiency and productivity, as is the autocratic leader. In addition, the democratic leader is also concerned about maintaining good group relationships in the organization. The democratic leader may be identified by the following workplace characteristics:

A feeling of open communications exists

Workers feel they are part of the organization

The leader is respected

Workers are self-motivated

Decisions are made at the lowest possible level

Efficient productivity is normal

Workers receive recognition and credit

There's a mutual desire for excellence

The leader doesn't proclaim infallible intelligence.

The democratic leadership style emphasizes support, understanding, participation, and involvement. The organization, when trained and operational, can function for extended intervals without the active presence of the leader. This leader activates, trains, and guides. He or she doesn't act as a full-time director.

The Non-leader Style

The non-leader style is also known as the free-reign style, the laissez-faire style, and any other name that implies abdication or fear of leadership in a leadership position. There are four reasons for this style:

1. Some leaders are appointed to those positions simply because a qualified person is not available. The assumption is that any leader is better than no leader.

2. Some leaders prefer to be specialists. They concentrate their full efforts on technical task functions and ignore the requirements of leadership.

3. Some leaders are too job security conscious. They fear that incorrect decisions or incorrect actions will cause them to lose their jobs. Consequently, they refuse to make those possible incorrect decisions that might result in a risky mistake.

4. Some leaders report to such overbearing and oppressive superiors they have no choice. That superior leader doesn't permit that subordinate leader to make decisions.

Although these are the three distinguishable leadership styles, they aren't completely clear and delineated. These styles overlap, so that a leader who acts predominately in one style will occasionally display those characteristics of another style. A leader may be classified only by his or her dominant characteristics.

Determinants of Leadership Style

Leadership styles don't just happen. If leadership were a born trait, leadership styles would by inherent. This is not the case.

Leadership is a learned process. That style to accompany leadership, by inference, is also a learned process. A person doesn't suddenly decide to change leadership styles from autocratic to democratic or vice versa. An attempt to suddenly change leadership styles might be hazardous, and counter-productive to organizational stability and productivity. The development, or a change, of leadership style is an evolutionary process guided by six influences. These include:

Background of the Leader

The background and life experiences of a person play an important role in determining that person's outlook toward workers and leadership. If the person was reared in an environment of cooperation, friendship, and sharing, his or her tendencies would be to carry that background into the work environment.

One with a social history of bickering, rivalry, and limited personality tendencies would most probably carry that approach into a work environment. That leader's opinion of people would also be a determining factor of the leadership style that he or she would develop.

A leader who believes people try to be efficient, supportive, enthusiastic and productive, would have a stronger tendency to rely upon the innate abilities of people. This would imply the leader would tend to be more democratic and supportive. Other leaders evolve into a feeling that workers cannot be trusted and must be driven and directed to perform their tasks. This feeling often becomes a catalyst for encouraging conflict in the workplace.

Leadership Training

Training is another important factor that determines a leadership style. Many training programs focus primarily upon those management considerations generally identified as scientific management. Scientific management considers those factors of productivity outside the concern of humanistic considerations. The effect of group and motivational influences wouldn't be a part of those scientific management considerations.

Concern of scientific management would include only factors of planning, process engineering, and statistical analysis to evaluate programmed actions. These statistical controls are categorized under the heading of management sciences. Leaders focused on training in the management sciences would tend to be less concerned about people motivations, suggesting the autocratic style would be the natural evolution.

Example of Superiors

Subordinate leaders are under pressure by their superiors to develop that superior's leadership style. That superior leadership style might be good or bad, right or wrong; but it's that superior's prerogative. Conflicting leadership styles between a superior and the subordinate cause frustration, reluctance, and apprehension by both leaders.

For example, a dominating autocratic senior leader would not understand the routine pace of a subordinate democratic leader. A democratic senior leader would question the insensitive tactics of an autocratic subordinate leader. This resulting pressure encourages the subordinate leader to emulate the style of his or her senior leader.

Expectations of the Company

Company policies and expectations influence, to some degree, a leader's style. An organization has its own life that produces policies and expectations. These policies and expectations are more fundamental than the level of influence top leaders in the company can control. Some of these influences are established by historical review, and others are assumed by individual perceptions. These expectations might be real or only imagined; nevertheless, they exist.

An organization that expects autocratic leadership from itself will ordinarily comply with that expectation. An organization known for more democratic styles will ordinarily encourage those more democratic styles.

Pressure from Associates and Peers

Some leadership styles are formed or influenced by peer pressure. A leader functioning with a democratic style could be misunderstood and intimidated by peers who recognize only 'good direct leadership.' Although it's unusual to acknowledge leaders are affected by the influence of peer pressure, it happens. Leaders are people, with personal feelings and emotions.

Actions of Subordinates

The leadership style of some leaders is influenced by that leader's subordinates. Some subordinates understand only one style of leadership, and that's the leadership style they expect. Some subordinates, particularly those from the underclass, want close personal direction, for that's all they understand. Unless they are told what to do, how to do it, and when to do it, they have no reason to do that task. In this example, a leader must be autocratic to gain productivity until untrained subordinates assimilate into the normal workforce.

Other subordinates might become so antagonistic against an extremely autocratic leader that the leader must become more democratic. This change is forced when the autocratic leader realizes subordinates have some influence that could affect that leader's job security.

Analysis of Leadership Styles

To reach maximum effectiveness, leaders must recognize that

subordinates are different. They have different backgrounds, different perceptions, different goals, and different aspiration levels. Even the relationships among workers in an organization are different. For example, one worker might be perceived as a great individual by some workers, while other workers might not even like that person.

Some workers are more comfortable and productive functioning in the environment of a democratic leader. This leader-worker combination is enhanced in a work environment that has alternative situations or conditions that require some degree of decision making by those workers.

Other workers are more secure and comfortable in an environment where they aren't required to commit themselves to make decisions. This would suggest that a repetitive task under the leadership of an autocratic leader would create a compatible work environment for these workers.

There's no real evidence to prove, or even suggest, that one leadership style directly creates more productivity than does another leadership style, particularly in the short term. However, the democratic style encourages more harmony and job satisfaction which may ultimately permit a more healthy and sustained workforce with less conflict.

Sources of Leadership Power

At this point one might ask, "What gives leaders the right, or the power, to lead?" According to two researchers, Raven and French, there are five basis, or influences, for this power to lead. Raven and French identify these five power influences as: legitimate power, coercive power, reward power, expert power, and referent power. Briefly defined, they are:

Legitimate Power. Legitimate power may be described as that power assigned to an individual by appointment to a designated superior position. That power is inherent to the position, not to the individual. For example, a manager's position has power over a supervisor's position. In reality, however, the supervisor could exhibit more personal power or influence.

Coercive Power. Coercive power is the influence based on fear. That fear may result from a person's perception, or it could be from actual threats or intimidation. Fear may attach to either position power or to personal power.

Expert Power. Expert power is established by a leader who is respected for his or her knowledge pertaining to a task. That leader is a recognized and respected specialist in the field or business he or she leads.

Referent Power. Referent power is also personal influence a leader earns by exhibiting characteristics accepted and respected by subordinates. These include honesty, integrity, and concerns for human welfare; or even boldness and courage.

Reward Power. Reward power is the influence one has to reward or compensate followers. This could be in the form of monetary rewards and compensation, or emotional rewards such as special recognition.

These power bases don't exist in isolation. Ordinarily, these power influences are interacting in combination to create a broad power base for a leader.

Leadership Behavioral Theories

Three leadership theories are routinely referenced during leadership training. Those theories will not be discussed in detail here; however, they will be briefly introduced to demonstrate their similarities:

The Continuum of Leadership Theory

This theory by Tannenbaum and Schmidt analyzes the relationship between a manager's authority and the freedom of a subordinate to make decisions. The conclusion is that managers may maintain their authority by defining the limits of subordinates' decisions. The greater the degree of decision-making the subordinate is permitted, the less direct authority the manager is required to exercise.

The Managerial Grid

Blake and Mouton developed a grid with a number scale of one to nine on intersecting horizontal and vertical lines. The horizontal line indicates the leader's concern for productivity. The vertical line represents the leader's concern for people. The point at which these extended numbers intersect indicates the type of manager.

For example, a manager identified as a 5,5 on the managerial grid would be average in consideration of both concerns. A manager identified as a 9,1 would be task oriented, but not concerned about people. A 1,9 manager would be concerned only about people. A manager identified as a 9,9 would be identified as one who is greatly concerned about people and productivity.

The Two-Dimensional Theory

This theory suggests that leadership has two factors that aren't necessarily mutually exclusive. They may be considered as separate entities. One of those factors is identified as *initiating structure*, which refers to job dedication and task focus. The other factor is called *consideration*. Consideration refers to the degree of people concerns, such as trust, respect, and understanding.

Review and analysis of these major leadership theories show they have a common major theme or association. That is, they all consider only two factors, which are productivity concerns and people concerns. Consistently successful leaders learn not only how to balance these two concerns, but also how to reach maximum levels of efficiency in each of those two factors of leadership. Those who fail to reach a maximum level, or at least an optimum level, of effectiveness in both factors eventually become a major source of conflict in their organizations.

Requirements of Leadership

Leaders often try to analyze or figure out their subordinates in attempt to increase their cooperation and productivity. Their analysis often turns to frustration. Before a leader tries to understand the motivations and actions of his or her subordinates, he or she must first analyze and understand himself or herself. Unless a leader understands his or her own motives, aspirations, fears, and position in life, then he or she will have great difficulty understanding and comprehending the motives and actions of others.

A Leader's Self-Analysis

To understand how to influence a work environment more positively to increase productivity by reducing conflict, the leader must review his or her background and aspirations. This review must be designed to determine any characteristics or traits that may circumvent positive efforts from producing a positive influence. A leader should analyze the following questions in his or her review process:

Rationality. Is the leader normally self- controlled? Or, is the leader overly excitable and overly reactive? Is he or she erratic, stubborn, or unreasonable?

Style. What's the leader's leadership style? Does the leader understand styles and their characteristics?

Dedication. Is the leader dedicated to results? Or, is the leader dedicated to other leaders or other outside interests?

Frustration level. Does the leader have clearly defined goals and aspirations? What is the leader's level of frustration when achievement of those goals becomes difficult?

Training. What is the degree and depth of leadership training of the leader? Has the leader had training in subjects of technical competency, success planning, and stress management?

Support. What is the level of support expected from superiors? What is the level of support given to subordinates?

Personal problems. Do normal personal problems exist, or are they high regarding financial, family, or substance abuse matters?

Before a leader tries to analyze other people's actions in the work environment, that leader must analyze himself or herself regarding these questions. The analysis of others will be guided by that leader's perception of himself or herself.

Leadership Requires Confidence

To be effective as a leader, that leadership demands confidence. Confidence should develop after objective self-analysis by a leader. During that self-analysis, the leader should identity his or her weaknesses and strengths. Every leader has some weaknesses.

Every leader also has many strengths. Those weaknesses should be targeted for improvement while the leader depends upon those strengths for confidence and results.

For example, a leader might recognize he or she is weak in the technology of his or her job requirements. The leader might also acknowledge he or she has good human relations skills. That leader should rely upon confidence of those human relations skills, while improving in the technical requirements. The leader shouldn't jeopardize his or her responsibility by focusing negatively on those weaknesses. From a practical viewpoint, no one is managerially strong in all areas of management functions. The leader must depend upon those stronger assets to remain more effective.

To maintain a high confidence level, a leader must also continue a personal development training schedule to reinforce leadership knowledge and confidence. Often, leaders become so absorbed by events of the moment they ignore the requirement to continue training to improve their value for the future. That training should include leadership training, personal development, and counseling methods. A leader who ignores enhancement training for himself or herself limits his or her potential for success.

That leader also limits the degree of success, productivity and profit that he or she may develop for that company; and, that leader also limits his or her ability to influence workers to improve themselves. Until a leader becomes perfect, personal development is essential. Are there any perfect leaders?

Understanding Human Relationships

For a leader to be efficient and reduce workplace conflict, he or she must understand people and their relationships. Problems that most often challenge a leader in the workplace are those problems caused by or result from human relationships. If the leader merely focuses his or her attention on methods and procedures designed to force productivity, that leader is ignoring the source of the greatest potential productivity gain, the human factor.

Although an understanding of human relationships is important to accomplish those functions of management: planning, organizing, coordinating, directing and controlling; there's another more important reason. This involves the concept of interdiction. Once relationship problems or difficulties occur, they ordinarily remain problems to some degree even after they're resolved.

For example, if two people strongly disagree regarding a workplace topic or procedure, the resentment and distrust between those two persons remain, even after that specific problem, or difference, is resolved. Interdiction is the process of recognizing and taking preventive action before a strong emotional crisis occurs to cause conflict.

Interdiction may occur only if the leader understands those relationships in his or her workplace. Those relationships create signals the leader must learn to recognize. Without understanding those relationship signals, the leader will focus on solving problems, rather than preventing problems.

Preventing problems has a more positive impact than does solving them. Preventing problems, however, can be accomplished only by understanding work environment relationships.

Leaders Must Consider Ecological Implications

The natural pressure on leaders forces them to focus almost exclusively on productivity and profit. Although it's unlikely a leader at any hierarchal level would wantonly create an ecological hazard that leader in his or her zeal to increase immediate efficiency and short-term profits might ignore an ecological event. The ecological disasters that exist from events of the past were most probably not diabolically planned by industrialists and leaders. Those disasters resulted from lack of timely technological knowledge, and from the competitive zeal of subordinate leaders to satisfy financial constraints placed upon them by their superiors.

Leaders can no longer ignore ecological considerations. They must seriously consider ecological implications of every decision and action. Although ecological concerns might not directly create specific conflict between workers and leaders in the workplace, there are situations when workers may be forced to carry out instructions by superiors to discard hazardous waste they believe is a violation of rules, ordinances, and regulations. In these cases, conflict might occur if workers are forced to do tasks that violate their values and beliefs.

Conflicts of Leadership

Leadership doesn't exist within a vacuum. There are many conflicts that influence the style, requirements, and considerations of a leader. As a leader develops, or as he or she changes environments, that leader must function within those policies and real or implied constraints of the organization. This analysis of leadership conflict will review those policies and individual constraints:

Established policies

Policies exist in organizations to prevent chaos, and to maintain normal order. They're designed to create guidance for decision-making, and to establish standardization that may result in fairness and equity. Policies are effective only if they are conspicuous and understood, otherwise there's no practical purpose for their existence.

Policies and procedures to guide the actions and conduct of people should consider the goals of the company, the managerial competency of the leader, and the needs of workers. It serves no purpose to establish a policy that's not related to company goals. Neither is it reasonable to create policies so complex or vague that leaders cannot enforce them because they cannot interpret them uniformly. Furthermore, to create policies that only restrict and limit activities of subordinates would create a clear signal to those people the company has no concern for their interests.

Ideally, subordinates should be allowed to participate in policy-making decisions that concern their physical and emotional well-being. Some employees have this freedom, not only as a signal of good faith by management, but also to include built-in motivators that may help the policies achieve their positive intent.

Constraints of Leadership

A major barrier that precludes the full development and use of leadership is that of leadership constraints. There are four serious constraints to leadership that must be considered. They include: fear of change, lack of effective delegation, the superior's defensive nature, and executiveship.

Fear of Change. Leaders are as fearful of changes they cannot interpret as workers are fearful of procedures they don't understand. For the worker, an accepted procedure has always worked, therefore it shouldn't be changed. From the leader's perspective, pertaining to that reluctant worker, the worker is simply irrational and stubborn.

Since there's ordinarily no one in higher positions to evaluate management's fear of change, it's simply acknowledged that the current system, or organizational plan, is normal and rational. The concerns of workers and leaders at lower levels of the organization are usually ignored, or considered by management as being normal organizational complaining. The typical subordinate's comment that leaders should consider is, "Why doesn't somebody do something?"

Somebody, senior management, must not routinely discount these comments as routine complaining by uninformed or uneducated lowly workers. Senior leaders must realize common sense and rationality isn't always dictated by intellectualism.

Lack of Effective Delegation. Delegation of responsibility and authority is a serious matter in most organizations. Traditionally, superiors freely delegate responsibility. Also traditionally, leaders only reluctantly delegate authority. The authority that's delegated by a superior rarely equals the responsibility the same superior demands of that subordinate.

Authority must, by reference, accompany responsibility. Without the necessary authority to fulfill or accomplish a responsibility, the assignment of responsibility is meaningless. More simply stated, responsibility is the task and authority is the tool to accomplish that task. Without an effective tool, the task is more difficult to accomplish. Many senior leaders are eager to assign their responsibility to a subordinate leader, but cannot force themselves to relinquish any of their authority. This reluctance to relinquish (delegate) authority has two bases:

First, the senior leader who refuses to delegate is an autocratic leader who's oblivious to motivators of subordinates. Secondly, the senior leader doesn't trust the decision-making ability of the subordinate leader. In either case, a serious problem exists that must be eliminated in the organization to perpetuate any degree of long term effectiveness.

Protective Nature of Superior Leaders. The defensive nature of many leaders doesn't permit, or allow, internal development of subordinate leaders. This reluctance by superiors to develop subordinate leaders to their full potential creates a natural conflict that produces a loss for the productivity system, and to the overall progress of a company.

An example of this requirement may be taken from the military system of leadership development. At any level of military leadership, the senior leader actively attempts to recognize potential future leaders under his or her area of influence. Those subordinate leaders who demonstrate potential for higher leadership positions are trained, groomed, and supported toward that leadership goal of sustainability. The ultimate aim is for the senior leader to insure his or her organization will not decrease in effectiveness during the absence or loss of that senior leader.

Non-military organizations don't actively share this same leadership development concept. Business organizations, in effect, purposefully don't use a system of planned replacements. From a practical standpoint, business organizations refuse to train subordinates who show signs of high leadership potential. There are two basic reasons for this reluctance to develop those high potential leaders.

First, the budget is considered. A leader being groomed for advancement would require a position and a title. The higher position and the higher title would require additional funding. This reason, however, is only minor in comparison to the second reason, which is basically the primary reason.

Secondly, leaders in business organizations tend to cling tenaciously to the security, financial rewards, and personal status of their positions. The higher the status, the more tenacious is the drive to maintain that position, or to advance within the same company. Consequently, a senior leader in a business organization has great difficulty with the leadership development concept of identifying and developing subordinate leaders with obvious potential.

The dominant leadership development concept in business is quite contrary to the military leadership development concept. Routinely, subordinate leaders in business organizations who attempt to show any extra or conspicuous leadership potential are treated with disapproval, contempt, jealousy, and rivalry by the superior who resents the competitive attitude.

This leadership conflict causes tragic loss of productivity, company growth and organizational harmony. Leaders with high leadership potential don't use that full leadership potential, for they recognize the superior leader's tenacious desire to remain unchallenged. Extraordinary leadership by a subordinate would be a challenge to that superior leader.

This conflict of leadership challenge might seem only theoretical. A simple review, however, of the numbers of higher level management positions filled by managers from outside a company quickly changes this concept from theory into fact.

Hiring to fill higher level positions, from outside the company, is de facto proof the company hasn't developed those potential leaders within the company. What other logical reason could deter or discourage the development of leaders within a company? Potential leaders exist in every company, but they are reluctant to show themselves.

The Executiveship Constraint. Executiveship is another serious constraint against effective leadership. Executiveship could be defined as considering all aspects and conditions of a problem, question or a situation, with intentions to take appropriate action - after all considerations have been reviewed, staffed, studied, and reconsidered. Executiveship doesn't require, nor does it permit, direct and definitive action by a leader.

Executiveship includes coordination, collaboration, thoughtful studies, serious conferences, multitudinous meetings, team effort, and a bulging attache case. The emphasis on executiveship becomes focused on itself, while the actual problem observes the flurry of activity from the last seat in the back row of the comedy club. Eventually, the problem or question disappears, or is welcomed into the organization by acquiescence and acceptance.

Summary - Leadership Constraints

These four leadership constraints continue as active deterrents against the development of efficient harmony that decreases conflict and improves productivity in organizations. These deterrents must be removed from leadership potential to permit full utilization of that vast reservoir of leadership capability that remains suppressed in business organizations. Leadership capacity is there in abundance. It must be exposed and developed.

Management and leadership must not continue to be only

words discussed as casual theory and vague concepts. Management and leadership are active words that have measurable life, meaning, purpose, and influence. Leadership is a determinant characteristic of productivity. Productivity is the basic foundation that permits the existence of business organizations. Business organizations require workers to fill jobs that are essential for people to earn income for survival.

If productivity declines, or doesn't remain internationally competitive, those workers will not have jobs, for those companies will not exist. A significant loss of competitive jobs in any country could eventually result in a decline in the standard of living for that country. The threat of a decline in the standard of living is real - it's not simply imaginary and theoretical. That threat, however, need not exist.

A major part of the answer to remove that threat is almost too simple to be recognized. Leaders should be trained to lead, and be allowed to lead without counter-productive constraints. If a fully supported leader cannot learn to develop a harmonious work environment and to execute productive leadership, that leader quickly should be replaced. Effective and productive employeeship shouldn't be expected until management has provided workers with real leadership.

Summary - Leadership Forces

In recent years, management has identified weak, unskilled, untrainable, and unmotivated workers as major excuses for conflict and declining productivity. These leaders also claim that foreign competition is unfair, as another excuse for their lack of competitive productivity.

American productivity hasn't improved because management created a work environment monster that's not only non-supportive of leadership efforts; that monster actually discourages inspired leadership efforts. Leaders aren't allowed to make decisions and accept accountability for their actions. Instead, they are ridiculed and chastised for not being *team members,* unless each question is staffed into oblivion. If a leader has the courage to make a reasonable decision he or she is labeled as ambitious and overly competitive. Leaders simply aren't permitted to be leaders.

It will certainly be difficult, if not impossible, to eliminate or to reduce workplace conflict, significantly, if leaders aren't allowed to lead on the basis of their own perspectives, perceptions, values, and ideals; assuming of course that those leaders are fundamentally competent.

A leader who must attempt the leadership process by artificially using the leadership traits of others cannot avoid conflict. That leader faces internal conflicts of those differing perspectives and values. The leader also creates conflict in the organization by not displaying a natural and sincere personality that he or she understands. If the leader cannot understand his or her own personality, values and position, then conflict with those to be led is inevitable.

4

EMPLOYEESHIP FORCES

The social and leadership consensus that leaders are responsible for worker motivation creates an ambivalent area that causes a continuing zone of conflict between leaders and workers. The purpose for this chapter is to clarify the association between worker motivation and personal worker success as they contribute to conflict and productivity in the workplace.

Basis of the Motivation Conflict

The ambivalence concerning the responsibility for worker motivation has been the fundamental cause of the lack of effective motivation in the workplace. Human relations leadership training, which uses the motivation theories of Abraham Maslow and Frederick Herzberg, implies leaders are responsible for 'applying' those motivational principles. Both theories, although not directly stated, imply leaders are ultimately responsible for creating conditions and taking actions to motivate their workers.

Other human relations researchers, theorists and writers have in fact, or by implication expressed a similar point of view. That point of view pertaining to motivation and productivity in the workplace is as follows:

The worker comes into the workplace with his or her own

cultural values, aspirations and perceptions. Since workers aren't supervisors or managers, they are therefore uninspired at least, and totally anti-management and anti-productivity at worst. Consequently, management must, in its great wisdom and ability, task itself to dominate or manipulate those workers to become motivated.

Although this concept of employee manipulation by management, by either human relations techniques or autocratic domination, might seem callous, it really isn't. Why? There are two basic reasons that make this manipulation concept a logical approach in some environments.

First, managers assume, and have been taught, that motivation techniques must be applied to encourage workers to act, to do something, and be productive. Consequently, management perceives itself as responsible for worker motivation. The management motivational tools to fulfill these responsibilities are autocratic actions, human relations techniques, and somewhere in between.

The second reason, or justification, for using these manipulative tools to motivate workers is that many workers really believe their destiny is a management responsibility. These workers create the need and justification for leaders to be forceful and manipulative, which becomes the source of conflict to the motivation question. The dilemma to the worker motivation question is that management accepts the requirement to motivate workers because many workers have acquiesced that as a management function.

Certainly, there are many goal-oriented and self-motivated workers who aren't included in this category. These goal-oriented workers would probably be effective and successful functioning under any work environment conditions or under any management style, for their self-image is larger than temporary barriers, including an atmosphere of uninspired leadership.

Motivation - Who's Responsible?

A basic question at this point is, 'Who is really responsible for employee motivation?'

The classicists might argue employee motivation might not be very important anyway, since job design and structural programming are the real productivity determinants. In this classical or traditional approach, workplace conflict and harmony are not considerations.

Human behaviorists might state or imply that since productivity's relationship to management's goals is the real issue, that management should be responsible for proper motivation to reach those goals. In this view, motivation would simply be another management function such as planning and organizing.

A dilemma is created by management's attempts to improve motivation in an organization. Although management usually accepts the responsibility to encourage policies and practices that will be motivational, and some workers accept those attempts as management's responsibility, some of those same workers resent management's attempts to manipulate them. They consider any rules and policies as overly restrictive, which inhibit their self-actualization and esteem needs; and they consider total freedom as an abandonment of management's responsibility to be in charge. This antithesis creates the workplace motivational conflict.

Under normal management theories, the burden of worker motivation is presumed to be the inherent responsibility of management. This assumption is as appropriate for participative management as it is for autocratic management. This is a basic assumption that's been an accepted situation since serious human relations management study began in the 1940s.

Why has this basic assumption not been challenged; since it's unreasonable to expect a supervisor or a manager tasked with front-line productivity requirements also to be a fully-trained and effective psychologist? Even trained and experienced psychologists aren't one-hundred percent effective in their specialty. Is it reasonable to expect more from a manager or a supervisor on the front lines trying to respond to superiors' demands for more productivity and increasing customer expectations, simultaneously?

What is management's role or responsibility in providing motivational environments for workers? Management's role must be to provide an environment, conditions, and opportunities for workers to motivate themselves. Management's role must be facilitative and supportive, not active and directive. Active and direct attempts to motivate workers tend to create defensive workers who become protective against the exploitation by management. Any real and meaningful motivation must be developed within each worker. For this development to occur, however, a new understanding and a new expectation must be created in the work environment.

That new understanding must be that workers are taught they, *not their leaders*, are responsible for their own motivation, since only they can determine what to do with their future. The new expectation must be that each worker will accomplish no more than he or she directly and explicitly plans to accomplish. Management's responsibility is to teach, encourage and enforce this new concept. This concept should be termed 'employeeship.'

Employeeship, at this time, is a non-existent word. The word doesn't exist in a regular dictionary. Yet, everything management does relating to personnel matters is guided and determined by the level of employeeship in an organization. Isn't it amazing that a word doesn't exist to describe the most significant part of an organization?

There are a few words that might suggest the possibility of the existence of employeeship. One of those words is leadership. The act and functions of being a leader, those things that leaders do, are identified as leadership. Leadership would imply leadership of something. That something that leadership influences is the implied employeeship. Leaders don't physically lead workers on the job. Leadership is performed by leaders leading that employeeship.

Another word that suggests employeeship is the word performance - employee performance. The word performance also fails as an adequate definition of employeeship. Performance is limited, in that it recognizes only a small part of employeeship. Performance may also be vague and clouded, for it's a characteristic that may be manipulated by the performer. The effect of performance is no better than it's perceived by the evaluation of the performance. Frequently, the evaluator is influenced in his or her evaluation by biases and prejudices. Even when performance is objectively evaluated, it's the result that's seen, not necessarily the employeeship that created the result.

Work ethic is another futile attempt to describe employeeship. Although the general implication of the idea of work ethic sounds profound, it's meaningless in terms of application. It's generally understood that work ethic describes one's approach and outlook toward work. It gives no clues of how to develop it, how to use it, or how the individual can derive any benefits from it. In one situation a good work ethic might mean blind subservience to a slave labor environment. In another situation, it could refer to a worker's zeal to become a supervisor. Work ethic has meaning only to the person who uses the word; consequently, it cannot be used to substitute as a definition for employeeship. A definition of the word employeeship should be given here:

> Employeeship encompasses all actions an employee takes in preparation for employment, and during the work process to contribute positive effort to an employer. That effort is designed to result in the employee's maximum efficient productivity for the employer, and fair wages and achievement factors for the employee.

This definition contains several concepts that must be analyzed. An understanding of this definition is imperative for leaders and workers to synthesize leadership and employeeship relations that influence conflict.

First, this definition implies an employee must plan to be an employee. A person must take positive action to prepare himself or herself to be ready to perform a task. If a job requires administrative or clerical skills, a person should train and prepare for those skills, before beginning the job. If the job requires manual labor, the person should prepare physically, before beginning the job. If the job requires customer interaction, the person should learn those communications skills before beginning the job. Employeeship begins with preparation.

Leadership also begins with preparation. It doesn't just happen. If one chooses to be an employee, he or she should prepare to practice professional employeeship.

Secondly, the level of employeeship is determined by the level of interest, focus, and positive effort one exhibits while performing the actual work process. This is the visible part of employeeship. This is the contractual portion of employeeship. The employer promises to pay the employee a stated amount of money. The employee, for that agreed amount, promises to give the employer his or her best efforts at that job. A weakness in either creates a zone of conflict.

Rarely does the employer default on the employer's part of the contract. On the other hand, rarely does an employee fulfill the employee's part of that contract. According to the source identified in Chapter One, authorities estimate the level of worker productivity is only fifty-percent.

Even if this estimate is in error by ten or fifteen percent, that lost productivity is still an unreasonable drain on the potential of our economy. This figure indicates workers choose not to fulfill their contractual promises, or they don't know how to practice professional employeeship. Or, perhaps they're still waiting for management to practice good motivation techniques, since management has assumed that self-imposed responsibility. Whatever the excuse, many workers fail in the productivity portion of employeeship. They refuse to accept their contractual (written, spoken or implied) promises.

Finally, regarding the implications in the definition of

employeeship, workers shouldn't only receive pay for their efforts, they should also receive feelings of achievement and satisfaction from those efforts. If they are fulfilling those requirements of professional employeeship, they will receive the positive rewards of those feelings. Feelings of achievement and satisfaction may result only if a person, employee or leader, knows he or she has earned the right to feel achievement and accomplishment. An employee who doesn't practice professional employeeship cannot understand the importance or the concept of this feeling of achievement. It can be understood only if it's been earned.

Effects of Employeeship

The quality of employeeship has more influence on the quality of the work atmosphere in a workplace than does the quality of leadership in a workplace. In effect, the quality of employeeship really determines the quality of a work environment. This concept is self-defining.

Leadership is a concept of actions designed to move other people to a predetermined goal or objective. If those other people are focused and performing efficiently toward that goal or objective, then leadership becomes irrelevant other than to define the goals and to provide the tools. The more good employeeship is exercised, the less leadership is required.

Conflicts result in a work environment when certain actions occur, or are absent. When employees avoid good employeeship, a leader must practice better leadership. Some leaders don't consistently know how to practice better leadership, for most situations are different in different environments. Consequently, leadership in some situations doesn't match perfectly to those environments. These situations usually cause some degree of discomfort and conflict between workers and leaders. Are these conflicts always the result of bad leadership? Or, could these conflicts be the result of bad employeeship?

Basic Requirements of Employeeship

The definition of employeeship given earlier in this chapter established the concepts, the rewards, and the demands to achieve employeeship. The definition, however, didn't indicate all the things necessary to develop employeeship. These specific requirements of employeeship are explained next to allow training by a concerned leader, or to allow a worker to do that for himself or herself. They include determination, personal values, and self-improvement.

Determination

The worker, the individual, is the one who is in control, and the only one who determines his or her level of success. Managers and supervisors have little direct influence upon a worker's overall success. This idea is contrary to strong beliefs by many people who consider their supervisors and managers as obstacles, blocking their way to higher levels and more pay. Supervisors cannot determine an individual's goals, prepare a person to reach those goals, and then actually do it for that person. This action must be done by each person, or each individual worker, for himself or herself.

Once a worker determines some meaningful goals, explained in Chapter Seven, that person must decide what to do and how to do it. That person must make a plan, or an outline, of step-by-step actions. These actions should be clear and specific so that person can easily understand each action required to become successful.

When the person has a clear outline, or plan, he or she must prepare to begin those actions. Preparing means to train, to become skilled, and to develop a positive mental state of mind. It also means to be in the right location so that reaching one's goals may be practical.

For example, if there are no factories in one's area, and that person wants to advance his or her career in a factory, then that person must move to a location where factories exist. If one wants to be a professional dog catcher, that person must go where there are dogs to be caught. If one plans to be a commercial fisherman, he or she must go where commercial fish are located. A person is not prepared if that person hasn't qualified himself or herself for a career and a location.

Only after a person has prepared himself or herself according to a plan is he or she ready to execute that plan. That person is then ready to do what he or she planned to do. That person is now in control of his or her destiny.

Personal Values

There are important guidelines, or principles, to follow if one plans to have a long-term, increasingly successful career. These principles require strong will-power and determination, for there are always reasons, excuses, and temptations to violate these principles. If one is not alert and prepared, he or she will learn to violate them from self-defensive actions to avoid responsibility, or to shift blame for errors or omissions.

It's better to understand these principles and apply them positively, than let usual negative tendencies automatically prevail. These principles include loyalty, dedication, and honesty.

Loyalty. The first principle is loyalty. There are many words used to describe loyalty. Some of these include faithful, supportive, stand behind, and indebted to.

Sometimes loyalty is a clear choice, and sometimes there are situations called split loyalties. Split loyalties would involve a situation where one must make a choice between two 'rights,' and one of those rights would have a negative impact upon the other. A good example of split loyalties in the workplace would concern those expectations from organized labor and from management, in those organizations that are labor influenced.

The loyalty question arises, should a union member support

his or her workplace to survive and be profitable, or should that person support his or her friends in the union? This question often causes such conflict that everybody loses in the process.

Also there are times when an action is not clear to differentiate between loyalty and disloyalty. For example, disloyalty would be considered an action which would have a negative effect upon a person that one is expected to support. Would remaining silent, not actively and aggressively supporting that person with relevant information, be considered disloyalty? Or, would it be considered as merely not taking a personal risk? The question of loyalty can be a clouded issue and, at times, difficult to determine a perfect answer.

The degree of loyalty that one exhibits will mark that person's career character. Loyalty is a subject that one should understand, so that person will not be categorized as *flaky,* as his or her career progresses. To consider loyalty, a person must also consider who and what to be loyal to. Loyalty considerations include:

•   **Loyalty to Oneself**

A person must be loyal to oneself if that person expects positive things to happen in his or her career. Being loyal to oneself means to prepare and support oneself mentally, emotionally, educationally, and intellectually. Before any of the other loyalties are relevant and can fit into their proper places, a person must understand this loyalty to himself or herself.

Mentally, one must know the definition and concept of loyalty. If not, it cannot be applied consistently. Emotionally, one must know himself or herself enough to prevent personal desires and perceptions from interfering with an understanding of conflicting situations. Educationally, one should be prepared to understand the conflicting situation, as it is, and not necessarily as it may be interpreted. Intellectually, one should take a step above the situation, and pretend to be an outsider looking on, to get a clear view of problems, reasons, and solutions. A person cannot effectively fulfill other loyalties until that person understands and is in control of his or her own self-loyalty.

• Loyalty to the Employer

A person must also be loyal to his or her employer. If for no other reason, there's an implied contract as a condition of employment that the employee will be loyal to the employer. An employee cannot rationalize enough, or find a reason or excuse large enough, to abdicate this loyalty and responsibility.

The employee makes a personal promise and commitment to be loyal. If that employee doesn't fulfill that obligation, eventually there must be corrective consequences.

First, if one is not loyal to the employer, then one hasn't been loyal to oneself. Consequently, that employee will earn the reputation of being *flaky* or *wishy-washy*. These are two common terms for changing ideas and loyalty back and forth as pressure dictates, at convenient times.

Second, an employee will probably lose his or her job. At the minimum, the employee will not experience normal promotions. Third, it may become difficult to find another job, for a person's reputation tends to follow.

• Loyalty to the Job

Finally, one should be loyal to the job. This is what the person prepared for, it's what the person applied for, and it's what the person earned. Under these circumstances it seems reasonable to suggest that the person should, therefore, appreciate and respect that position.

Being loyal to one's job, in essence, means to be a good worker - to be a good employee. It means to do what the person said he or she would do when the job was earned. Job loyalty has many demands, some of which require focused effort.

1. An employee should be to work on time. This is a critical and high-tension subject in almost all work environments. Being late to work, frequently, has several implications. It implies the worker feels no responsibility for the work. It implies the worker doesn't care if co-workers must work harder to cover for that tardiness. It implies the worker doesn't care if the company loses productivity. And, it implies the worker thinks those supervisors aren't competent enough to resolve the tardiness problem. All these implications, whether valid or not, cause tension and friction that generates conflict.

2. An employee should be an efficient worker. Some workers appear busy all the time, yet they accomplished nothing. This is another common job disloyalty action. Sometimes it's intentional; sometimes it's unintentional. When a worker accepted a job he or she agreed to be efficient and to produce something. The worker did not agree or promise simply to be there and to act busy. There might be some jobs that have this strange requirement, but that would be an extraordinary situation. Most jobs have an accomplishment or a productivity requirement.

A worker should ask himself or herself at the end of each work day if he or she accomplished anything that day. If the answer is "yes," then that person should feel proud of that accomplishment. If the answer is "no," then that worker should plan to change that for the next work day. That person should prepare a list of things to do that will result in some accomplishment that will result in a personal feeling of achievement.

3. The employee should be a perceptive worker. An employee also has a duty to know what's happening in the work environment to help identify errors and mistakes that might reduce profits in the company. The employee should also be aware of events, to make suggestions for improving conditions or operations. The comment, "I don't know, I just work here," is one of the most blatant and conspicuous indicators that the person who makes that remark doesn't

comprehend the full scope of his or her loyalties and responsibilities. An implication of that comment is that the employee is not concerned with his or her work environment. Of course, the comment could mean other things as well, such as an attitude problem or a personality deficiency.

A perceptive employee knows his or her responsibilities, duties, and loyalties. That employee strives to fulfill those basics, not only by direct work effort, but also by improvements and enhancements. That employee should seek more efficient and effective methods to improve his or her organization.

4. The employee should be friendly. This obligation is often disregarded by workers, supervisors, and managers. Although managers and supervisors should set an example for this requirement, it's equally the responsibility of each individual worker. Workers are in the workplace approximately eight hours daily, therefore each should do his or her part to insure the workplace is comfortable and friendly.

To have that environment friendly people must create it and maintain it. It's difficult to maintain a comfortable and friendly environment, free of conflict, if only one person is anti-social or unfriendly. All workers, supervisors and managers are equally responsible to help create and maintain a friendly place to work, so their energies may be concentrated to efficiently accomplish tasks that create productivity.

5. An employee should be helpful. When anyone on the job needs assistance or information, a fellow employee is obligated to give that assistance. A worker shouldn't stand or sit idly by waiting while co-workers are busy or over-burdened. Getting the over-all job accomplished is everyone's responsibility.

This is another work situation that creates conflict and disharmony in a work environment. If all employees don't contribute toward the common goal, then some employees feel overburdened.

This causes anxiety, choosing polarized positions, and conflict. To avoid the possibility of this negative response, an employee should strive to be helpful and considerate.

There are some environments where this helpful assistance is discouraged. One would be in an organization of over-specialization. In over-specialized environments, only specifically assigned individuals may work at a specifically designated job. This condition discourages the source of job enhancement and job enlargement considerations.

Some labor-management contracts also prohibit job sharing or job diversity. This is another of those unnatural and artificial conditions that result in lost productivity, an over-priced product, elimination of a source of achievement and workplace conflict. Neither of these conditions is conducive to help fulfill an employee's feelings of achievement, accomplishment, or contribution in the workplace.

Many loyalties exist in the workplace that must be recognized and fulfilled. Some of these loyalties directly affect the productivity of a company that may ultimately determine whether or not a company continues to exist. The continued existence of that company is important not only to that company, it's equally important to people who need jobs to survive and to continue a success plan.

There are other loyalties that must be recognized more personally by an individual. These are the loyalties that eventually determine or expose the basic character of a person, and influence the harmony or disharmony in the work environment.

Dedication. Another principle of employeeship is dedication. This includes dedication to the job, dedication to excel, and dedication to be number one. One cannot and will not perform at his or her best if he or she is not dedicated to the task. One cannot give a hundred percent toward maximum performance. To be dedicated to one's job, a person must accept the requirement of that job as his or her personal duty.

Everything a person does efficiently enhances his or her self-image, reduces the cost of a company's products or services, reduces workplace conflict, and makes products or services more competitive in the market place.

There's a strong tendency among average workers to do just enough to get by or to do only what they think is expected of them. These are the workers who perform at only fifty percent of their capabilities. Many workers don't realize the more dedicated they are, the more they contribute, the more probable is their achievement of higher success. Those workers will advance no further in their careers than they are willing to contribute in dedicated performance.

A worker who is sufficiently dedicated will have a burning drive to be the best he or she can be on the job. That person will not be personally satisfied unless he or she is number one in performance, or at least number one to the maximum of his or her ability.

One who understands the value of good employeeship constantly strives to set a positive example in his or her work environment. Doing just enough to get by would be embarrassing for this person.

Honesty. Honesty is another important principle of employeeship one must exhibit at all times. Nobody likes a dishonest person, especially in a workplace where it cannot be tolerated. Dishonesty destroys feelings of mutual respect and creates apprehension and frustration. A worker cannot afford to do anything that will be even partially interpreted as dishonesty.

Dishonesty isn't limited to major theft. It also includes little things, such as taking pens and paper from the office, without authorization. It includes more important and personal things, such as making false statements about someone at the workplace, or not giving truthful or complete information to other people who need information to make decisions. Not giving one's best efforts on the job, after having made a contract to do so, is also an act of dishonesty.

An employer is owed honesty the same as the employer is owed loyalty. It's part of the employment contract even if it's not specifically written. Honesty is not something an employee can arbitrarily decide for himself or herself, based upon his or her dislike of management or working conditions.

The individual person, the worker, is the only one who is responsible for reaching goals he or she sets for himself or herself. That person is the one in control. He or she is in the driver's seat. Whether that person pursues those goals or not will be decided only by his or her self-determination. Nobody else will, or can, do it for that person. Furthermore, no one else should have the right or the responsibility to determine that person's personal success. Experiencing the process of success is much of the reward.

Self Improvement

Everyone is for self improvement. No one ever says self improvement is not a good plan. Everyone agrees that self improvement is a good thing that everybody should do, especially another person.

Many people say they plan to take a course or train toward some career to improve themselves - *someday.* How many of those people actually follow through on their plans for that course or that training? Why do those good intentions to pursue personal self improvement rarely become actual events? Why do so many people fail to do those things they're planning to do?

Self improvement will be discussed here to help reinforce its importance and to identify reasons that discourage people from starting. People need continuing self improvement for three important reasons:

Understanding.. One needs a steady flow of ideas and information for enlightenment. One's mind works at higher efficiency and excitement when it's learning new things it can assimilate. The more information one has, the faster this assimilation process can occur. This is the basis for the narrow view and limited personality of people in the lower social classes. Their lack of positive self development limits their ability to interpret new information.

Happiness. There are many self improvement methods and sources that can give a person much personal joy and satisfaction.

Career. Constant self improvement is the most positive way to advance one's career.

Barriers

Since people recognize self improvement is a good thing, why are so few doing it? Why do workers, and others, wait for something to happen without using free time to improve themselves? Is there not some degree of guilt by letting that time waste away? What's the reluctance?

This hesitancy is created by *barriers* to self improvement. These barriers are the real and imagined reasons that allow a person to avoid taking the first step. These barriers are easy to identify and categorize. They include:

Lack of incentive. One doesn't need more self improvement. The person's career is progressing, so why should that person do something that's not necessary?

Doubt. The fear of failure at trying to do something new or different.

Loss of freedom. The dislike of being forced into a time schedule.

Too busy. Not having enough time to do everything.

Cost. Not having enough money to buy books or pay for classes.

Selectivity. Not having the right courses or the right books available.

Do any of these barriers sound familiar? Everyone has good reasons and excuses for not doing something. That's one of the human traditions. Many of these barriers are also real, and present real problems to people who attempt to improve themselves.

Acknowledging these barriers, what can one do to begin a self improvement program? First, one must recognize that getting started, just taking the first step, is the most difficult part. A person must face this part head-on, for there is no alternative way to begin.

One must decide to do something, and then actually do it. In deciding what to do, however, people have alternatives. There is some flexibility to overcome those barriers of lack of time and money. That flexibility is possible because there are two general categories of self improvement methods; the formal method, and the informal method.

The formal method consists of taking classes or training in certain subjects or activities. Here one would attend a formal class or seminar to gain knowledge. The formal method would most likely include a grading procedure.

The informal method includes self-study, or self-training. The most basic method of self-study is simply to read an appropriate book.

The informal method is acceptable for self improvement under certain conditions: that a degree or certificate isn't required, and, that one has enough self-discipline to continue a steady and consistent study program. If a person doesn't have the time or money to attend formal classes, then this method of study is certainly a reasonable alternative. In any event, it's better than doing nothing. Furthermore, it's taking that first step one must take to practice self improvement. Once a person takes that first step, other steps become easier. Those next steps will probably happen automatically.

Assume that a person understands the reasons for continued self improvement and that person knows there are formal and informal methods. He or she is ready to begin. An obvious question becomes, "What subject should be taken?" The answer to that question depends upon the time limit one anticipates, and the level of technicality in the present or planned job for that person.

If one's career is in a technical field, and that person wants to improve technical qualifications, then logically he or she would begin with a technical course. Or, one could begin by reading technical books or other publications related to that career field. Depending upon one's long range goals, a person might decide, eventually, to add studies that would prepare for supervisory or management possibilities. This would include study in communications and leadership.

Persons who have clerical and administrative jobs would probably want to begin their studies with office skills and communications skills. They too would want to branch out into other career broadening studies after they were confident with those basics.

There are also general knowledge books. These books cover every conceivable subject. These books, although ordinarily read for the simple pleasure of reading, add to a person's storehouse of knowledge which helps put ideas and questions into perspective.

Another category of books, or study, that's often overlooked is that pertaining to personal development. These studies don't concentrate on any specific career specialty. Instead, they concentrate on helping one to understand oneself in relation to his or her environment. These are valuable studies, pertaining to subjects such as; stress management, positive thinking, handling crisis, and relaxing. These studies or books shouldn't be overlooked in planning one's self improvement agenda. One should not forget that this source of study is free; books are available in libraries.

Self improvement is a critical factor in achieving success. One cannot expect to be successful if he or she doesn't give reasonable effort to reach that goal. Competition is keen for those few opportunities that become available. If a person is not ready and better prepared when those doors open, that person will not reach his or her goal. Someone else will have prepared himself or herself better and will claim the prize before an unprepared person even finds the right race track.

A good employee should always be ready and should keep improving his or her knowledge and abilities. One shouldn't lose the race because he or she couldn't find the race track.

Summary

Workplace conflict is an illusive quality that refuses to allow itself to be eliminated. Most competent leaders prefer to work in environments without conflict that generates problems where there should be none. Workers also prefer to work in environments that are friendly, facilitative, and personally rewarding. Yet, rarely does this desired level of harmony and cooperation exist. Conflict dominates relationships in most work environments simply because a consensus has never been reached to determine the exact cause of conflict. Without determining the real cause, or causes, things cannot be corrected, including workplace conflict.

Traditionally, it's been customary and stylish to blame leaders for most, if not all, workplace conflict. Many management trainers, seminar leaders, management consultants, and writers rely upon this traditional view. They even reinforce this view as the basis of their livelihood by writing and teaching those views that are considered acceptable.

This view is a bandwagon approach since it's the socially rational and acceptable view. The idea that workers are also responsible for that conflict isn't supported, since the assumption that leaders are responsible for workers' personal motivation is the socially acceptable approach.

Focus on workers as a source of workplace conflict would also be less profitable for those people who rely on management training for their incomes. Over ninety percent of the money spent on training in industry is spent on management and leadership training. The small amount of money that's spent on worker training is spent only for technical training. There is no economic incentive to identify ordinary workers as an equal contributor to conflict in the workplace. That's not a financially profitable approach for training.

Workers, however, are part of the work environment. In fact, they're the largest part of the work environment. Since they are a large part of the work environment, and since they are living, breathing, and rationally thinking members of that environment, they have the power to make decisions and choices that affect the quality of their lives. They also have the power to affect the level of conflict in their work environments.

In most cases the intelligence levels of workers are the same as the intelligence levels of leaders. Only training and experiences are different. This suggests workers have the mental ability to make choices in their attitudes, their motivations, and their career design and development.

The concept of *employeeship,* briefly defined in this chapter, is to assign the responsibility for personal motivation where it belongs - to each individual - whether that individual is a leader or a worker. One person cannot and should not be responsible for another person's career plans and career development.

Since the concept of personal responsibility for employeeship is so foreign from traditional beliefs and social acceptance, however, leaders must accept the responsibility to train their subordinates in that concept of employeeship. Perhaps society might recognize this necessity, eventually, and employeeship will become part of the normal education process in public school systems.

Although employeeship has many requirements and considers

many factors, only three requirements of employeeship have been specifically identified in this chapter. Other requirements and factors of employeeship are identified throughout this book, many of which are shared with leadership requirements.

5

OTHER CONFLICT FORCES

The two previous chapters identified forces and influences that tend to promote conflict in work environments. Chapter Three identified many weaknesses of leadership that promote conflict. Chapter Four outlined the concept that workers tend to create conflict by their lack of personal plans to motivate themselves to be successful.

This chapter will analyze other forces and influences that also contribute to conflict in the work place. These forces are not specifically applicable to either leaders or workers. In most cases they may be applicable to both. Consequently, these forces will be analyzed as general conditions of the workplace that must be considered by leaders and workers. These forces may also be considered to eliminate conflict in other social environments outside the workplace. They include:

- Personality

- Consideration and Courtesy

- Pride and Self-image

- Changes

Although some of these topics are related, they will be

analyzed separately as individual concepts.

Personality

A person's personality has much influence on the frequency of conflict one will encounter. Communications and personal interactions are no different in the workplace than they are in general society for they involve people interacting with other people. The workplace is usually more sensitive to the influence of personalities since the workplace ordinarily involves a more concentrated level of interactions. Furthermore, those interactions are usually biased by individual self- interests.

In a workplace those personality interactions aren't used merely for casual conversation and social chit-chat. Individual personalities expose themselves in the process of coordinating, directing, training, instructing, and gathering information in the normal flow of the work process.

Leaders must communicate with workers during those leadership functions; and the way they communicate through their personalities directly affects a worker's response. It's not uncommon for a worker to say, "I don't mind my boss telling me what to do, I just don't like the way he says it." Neither is it unusual for a leader to say, "John's a good worker, but he has an attitude problem."

Neither of these conditions has a direct influence on the actual work process. The opinion of the other party that results from these reactions, however, directly affects the harmony in a workplace that creates an impact, usually negative, upon the work process. Let's consider a typical example of the influence of personality on the normal work process in an average workplace.

Jeff has been working in the produce department of a large grocery store for about two years. His manager, Janice, was confident and comfortable in her job, and she displayed her confidence in her association with her subordinates in the store. Jeff enjoyed his conversations, whether job related or casual, with Janice for she always made Jeff feel at ease with her smile, her friendliness, and her obvious effort to help Jeff and other workers feel comfortable and important.

Jeff was proud of the way he kept the produce in his department, for it was always fresh and blemish free and neatly arranged. He was especially proud of the way he kept the various bright colors of the fruit and vegetables color coordinated to create more eye appeal. That made his department look friendly. Janice would often tell Jeff, "Your department always looks so good I could almost live here."

To insure Janice was pleased, Jeff always looked for better ways to display the produce so that it would be more attractive, not only to Janice, but also to customers who would buy more to help him keep his supply constantly changing so that fresh produce was always on display.

When Janice was promoted to regional manager, she was replaced as the store manager by Wayne. Wayne had been an assistant store manager at another store for over two years. Wayne was anxious to become a store manager, not only for more pay, but also to show what he could really do.

Wayne was different from Janice. Janice had an outgoing personality that permitted her to casually interact with people, and in most cases be the initiator of most of the conversations. She seemed concerned about people's feelings, and obviously attempted to make those around her feel more comfortable with themselves and their environment.

Wayne was more withdrawn. He seemed to be in deep thought most of the time and often would barely acknowledge a greeting of "hello" or "good morning." Even when he acknowledged a greeting, that acknowledgment usually appeared insincere and forced. Workers at the grocery store, including Jeff, realized that Wayne simply wasn't a friendly person.

After Wayne had been in the store for two months, Jeff felt

he should try to interact more with Wayne. Most of the time when Wayne came through the produce department, he seemed to be in a hurry, on a more important mission, and Jeff had not felt secure enough to stop him to ask questions or to initiate casual conversation. Jeff decided he would take this bold step, for he wanted to learn what Wayne liked or disliked in produce presentation. He wanted to feel comfortable that he was doing it the way Wayne wanted it. He also really wanted some praise, for he knew that he had the best produce department in the city.

That afternoon Wayne came toward the produce department and Jeff noticed that Wayne didn't seem to be in a great hurry. This was Jeff's opportunity. As Wayne came within hearing range, Jeff made eye contact with Wayne and said, "Wayne, I have a question for you if you have a moment." Wayne replied, "Sure, what do you want?"

Jeff explained to Wayne that he had been at the store for two years in the produce department and really wanted to keep improving his department. He asked if Wayne had any ideas on how he might make it better, based upon his experience at other stores. Wayne responded, "No, not really. This looks okay to me. Just make sure you keep the floor cleaned so no one slips on a rotten vegetable or a smashed grape." Wayne continued to walk on through the produce department as he was talking.

This response was doubly embarrassing for Jeff. He knew he never allowed dropped produce to remain on the floor; and more importantly, Wayne didn't seem interested in talking to him, after Jeff had the courage to initiate the conversation. Jeff's interest and enthusiasm toward his job declined after that encounter, for Jeff felt that Wayne didn't care enough to earn Jeff's extra efforts. This was the beginning of conflict, for Jeff no longer felt that his manager deserved his cooperation and his best efforts.

This example shows that personality by a leader can influence a worker to be pro-productivity or anti-productivity. Since productivity is the fundamental basis that determines the level of workplace conflict, then it's reasonable to associate personality directly with workplace conflict.

Although management theorists might suggest management actions and reactions refer to management style, a manager's personality may be contradictory to a leaders planned leadership style. Some leaders who try to use a human relations leadership style aren't aware personality is the real force that permits that style. Simply refusing to be dictatorial and offering subordinates more motivational opportunities, the basics of human relations leadership, isn't enough to allow the full potential of subordinates to develop.

The leader's personality is the force that brings all those positive qualities together to encourage the highest performance and productivity. A leader's personality shouldn't be considered synonymous with leadership style.

Although the example above focuses on a leader's personality, the personalities of workers are equally as important. A worker's personality might even be more important for the success of that worker than any affect it has in one specific workplace. Ordinarily, a leader's personality might be somewhat disregarded if that leader's personality doesn't conflict with his or her superior, or the organization. A leader's weak or negative personality ordinarily becomes a handicap only to the productivity of his or her organization. Ordinarily it doesn't jeopardize that leader's career. Although that productivity might not be at it's highest potential level, history demonstrates mediocrity is sufficient in most organizations, so long as a reasonable level of profit continues for the company.

As long as the search for and acceptance of mediocrity continues in our business and industrial society, neither leadership nor employeeship will ever be fully developed. Under this handicap workplace conflict will, therefore, most likely continue to be the natural order.

A worker's personality, on the other hand, is considered an important factor in his or her career potential. A worker with a personality considered undesirable by his or her superior is often labeled as a person who has an attitude problem. Not only do leaders lose their desire to communicate with a person with an attitude problem, often these differences of attitude and personality are documented on the worker's performance report. Those performance reports are often the basis for pay raises and promotions within the company. These opinions and recordings occur even if a worker's negative personality is created by management actions.

The cause of a worker's personality or attitude problem is rarely, if ever, considered. This generates more conflict, for a worker ordinarily feels trapped in an environment where he or she has no recourse to resolve problems.

Consideration and Courtesy

There's a mirror effect for each person as he or she functions within society. One faces a mirror when that person takes any action or makes any comments that affect the goals or self-respect of another person. Each person faces a mirror with all that person's actions, comments, and even attitudes.

Many people are somewhat aware this mirror effect exists. This awareness is expressed through statements such as: "As you sew, also shall you reap." "You got what you asked for." And, "What goes around, comes around." These comments often are accepted without thought or analysis to their full meaning. These statements are used to philosophically justify an event, or to glibly shrug off lengthy justifications.

It's important to acknowledge this mirror effect particularly to reduce or eliminate conflict in the workplace. Anything one does in the workplace usually is returned in an increased magnitude. A person who is courteous and helpful will ordinarily find the workplace has less conflict that will interfere with his or her goals of financial success and happiness.

Happy and successful people understand this mirror effect and they use it effectively. Those who are happy and successful may not identify their life philosophy as the mirror effect; nevertheless, they apply those principles. Anyone can use this concept to improve the quality of his or her life in areas of happiness, success, and financial growth.

The mirror affect concept is easy to learn, and fun to apply. A person cannot be successful and happy if he or she doesn't use this concept at least to a reasonable degree. The only realistic alternative to using the mirror approach is to be a greedy, grumbling, complaining, and self-centered grouch. The grouch usually isn't happy being unhappy unless he or she is making someone else just as miserable. Conflict clings to and is part of the atmosphere that surrounds a grouch.

Consideration and Courtesy - the Basis

The basis for the mirror effect are the words consideration and courtesy. This concept will be explained further. First, however, specific definitions for those words, consideration and courtesy, are necessary.

Consideration is an emotional trait or a psychological feeling that a person possesses. A person uses this trait or feeling to form a reaction to events that the person hears, sees, or perceives.

Courtesy is the outward response, or result, from the person's consideration. Courtesy, the action, is guided by consideration, the feeling.

Courtesy and consideration don't always function in unison. A person may be considerate of others, and yet not know how to express that consideration by an act of courtesy. This inability to openly express courtesy is a common cause of conflict in many situations, because a person's real thoughts and intentions aren't easily expressed, especially if that person is overly introverted or shy. Conversely, a person may be forced to be openly courteous, without any inner feelings of consideration.

Consideration feelings and courtesy acts must be identified as one unit to use the mirror effect as a practical tool to increase harmony and to reduce or eliminate conflict. There's no description, at this time, for this single unit. To permit further analysis this combined consideration and courtesy unit will be defined as a "view," which is, basically, one's general outlook on life.

There are two of these defined views to consider. One is the good view. The other is the bad view. The good view is comprised of high levels of consideration and courtesy. The bad view, naturally, is comprised of low levels of consideration and courtesy.

To practice good leadership or good employeeship, one must know how to use the good view. This is necessary if a worker or a leader chooses to become happy and successful. Using these good views of consideration and courtesy is a pleasant and enjoyable experience. With practice it's a simple process that develops automatically.

An Example

Pretend you are approached by a fellow employee, worker or leader, you dislike. You cannot stand the sight of him, you cannot stand the sound of him, you cannot stand the smell of him, you cannot stand the presence of him. You really don't like this guy! Nevertheless, you work with this person so you must communicate with him and coordinate with him. How should you accept this person and react to his presence?

This is the perfect time and situation to practice the mirror approach to avoid conflict. That conflict might be open and hostile or it might be subdued, since you realize you should treat a fellow person with common respect. You know you don't like this person. That person probably knows you don't like him. Consequently, open communications between both will probably be difficult.

When approached, visually pretend you have a giant mirror

with you. You place the mirror between yourself and the other person so that you see your reflection in that mirror. Now, which of your views will you use? Will you use the good view, or the bad view? Will you want to project good things at yourself, or will you want to treat yourself badly?

Since most people prefer to be treated with courtesy and respect, one would expect that same treatment for oneself, from oneself. How can a person show dislike for someone if that person is looking at the other person as if he or she were looking at himself or herself?

This same mirror effect is equally useful in all areas of one's life. It applies to sharing of time, resources, enthusiasms, and the enjoyment of just living. If one enjoys those things then that person should enjoy sharing those things with one's other self in that mirror even more. If a person is sharing with that other self how can that person not be receiving something in return?

Although the mirror effect is applicable in all areas of one's life, it's especially important in the work area. Many people spend more time with their co-workers than they do with any other group, including their families. Since they spend so much time with co-workers, the atmosphere and job environment have strong impacts on their lives.

Imagine how productive, rewarding, and fulfilling a job environment could be if all workers, supervisors, and managers used their mirrors with good views throughout each day. Communications would be clear and sincere, instructions would be cordial, directions would be goal oriented, and employee interactions would be friendly and open. Managers and supervisors would say "hello" or "good morning" first to employees to help those employees feel relaxed and comfortable, not apprehensive and intimidated. All employees would be diligent in their actions for they would understand those actions are appreciated and respected.

An employee will receive more than he or she gives, if that

employee uses his or her mirror diligently and honestly. One might not receive exactly what's expected, or when it's expected. One might feel he or she is doing all the sending, with no positive responses from the mirrored self. Then, when least expected, that person will be more financially comfortable, more successful, and more fulfilled with the enjoyment of understanding life's real events.

The Value of Courtesy

Courtesy is not a trait or a requirement that should be taken for granted, or superficially considered in a work environment. Courtesy is the real key that unlocks the potential and possibilities of all other elements and functions in a work environment. Without courtesy, other functions cannot operate smoothly, a characteristic that's paramount to workplace success.

Courtesy is so crucial for eliminating conflict in a workplace that it must be considered the oil to success and productivity. Without that oil to reduce friction, the moving parts of a work environment will not operate smoothly and efficiently to permit maximum performance.

Pride, Ego, Self-Image

Pride, ego and self-image are dominating personal forces. They affect personality, rationality, decision-making, and one's ability to interact with other people. There's no area of a person's daily activity and decision-making that's not influenced to some degree by pride, ego, and self-image.

Traditionally, we are taught that pride and ego are negative characteristics. This creates the impression that one must act subdued and passive to be regarded as a 'good person.' This general impression isn't necessarily valid. Pride and ego can be negative or positive, depending upon how they're recognized and used. It also depends upon one's definitions of those terms. Those definitions might not match the historical manner of use or misuse of those words. Let's consider a closer analysis of those two important words as they apply to normal workplace conflict:

Pride

Is pride something a person should avoid? Is it something only a few people have? Is it applicable only to rich people, poor people, obese people, or thin people? Is it something one could find or lose instantly; something that's here today and gone tomorrow? Is pride considered a positive trait or is pride merely a label for other characteristics considered negative, which might include: stubborness, hard-headedness, pig-headedness, and nonconformist? To answer these questions, one must understand the definition and meaning.

When a person is described as a proud person, he or she is usually considered one who's not flexible in personal or social adaptation. The concept of pride has been associated with the antisocial behaviors of stubbornness, hard-headedness, and pig-headedness. These terms should be labeled and called exactly what they are: stubborness, hard-headedness, and pig-headedness. These traits are defensive mechanisms by people who aren't open-minded enough, or who don't possess enough self-presence or self-confidence to use rationality in reaching conclusions.

Real pride, on the other hand, is something that emerges from a person's character. It manifests itself in feelings of accomplishment or satisfaction at achieving something or in overcoming a difficulty. It's positive reinforcement that tells a person he or she has succeeded, and can reach higher successes.

A person's accomplishment will speak louder, more clearly, and more positively than any words a person might utter. Those accomplishments will grow within one's inner self and show themselves in the attitude and approach one takes toward life. This pride will be manifested in one's presence and will allow that person to reject conflict and despair, and to seek only those harmonious events that create more success. A person who possesses real pride, and understands its significance, will reject those situations that breed disharmony and conflict. A person who possesses pride is too busy using that pride to create more success to worry about the minor annoyances of life that may generate only conflict and failure.

Pride, real pride, should be generously shared with family members and close friends. Sharing the pride of accomplishment with friends is part of friendship and should be respected. Real friends can share those things without feelings of touting, bragging, or jealousy. One's accomplishments become his or her friends' accomplishments, for they share that feeling of pride. Close friends can develop inspiration and pride within themselves, by knowing someone close to them can achieve success. One reinforces his or her pride from friends, while at the same time, those friends see a higher level of aspirations for themselves.

There's another trait identified as pride that should be understood to differentiate it from real pride that's a positive asset. The other pride, false pride, could also be called judgmental pride. False pride is not pride at all, only a form of jealousy that creates disharmony and conflict.

How does one detect false pride? It can be identified and analyzed only by its symptoms. False pride is exhibited by a person who makes comparative judgmental analysis of other people's actions. These people who exhibit false pride are superior to everyone else because: they think better than other people, they are more intelligent than other people, they do more things than other people, they take more trips than other people, they derive more pleasure from their trips than other people, they belong to more groups than other people, they have more friends than other people, and they have only select, special people as their friends.

These are people who compare themselves to others, and in their comparison they are always better or superior. This superior position gives them not only the right, but the duty, to analyze and judge other people's actions. This action doesn't express pride. It expresses jealousy; or, maybe even a superiority complex or another form of psychological or social illness.

Real pride is a positive trait. Pride is a positive feeling toward oneself about an accomplishment that the person has achieved. It creates incentive, encouragement, and reinforcement to accomplish more, so that a person can maintain a feeling of pride at a high level.

One should be proud of what he or she does to improve himself or herself. That's the essence of pride.

Ego

Ego is another word with a vague meaning. Ego, as in pride, is a word that's generally associated with negative qualities. Ego also is an overused and misused word. Instead of using the word ego to describe those negative personality flaws, one should use those words that describe exactly what they are: superiority complex, overbearing nature, compulsive talker, discourteous person, or perhaps a socially untrained person.

Ego has a different meaning. Briefly described, according to psychologists, ego is that subconscious part of people that makes them approach life rationally and in a controlled manner. If it were not for the subconscious ego, another part of one's subconscious would let a person do wild and crazy things. Ego is the thermostat that keeps a person's actions under rational control. When one gets too docile or too wild, the ego (thermostat) forces that person back into a range that's acceptable to the subconscious.

Pride and ego are good qualities. One must acknowledge, of course, the pride and ego that's been described. One should acknowledge that pride is a feeling of accomplishment that feeds itself on more accomplishment. Ego is a necessary function that one's subconscious mind uses to keep a person within a reasonable range of motives and pursuits. Ego is not synonymous with superiority or snobbishness. Personal pride and ego are the two essential components that permit a person to develop the universally desirable quality of a good self-image.

Self-Image

Ordinarily, a positive and productive person is one described as having a good self-image. That person is not usually described as being a person with a high level of pride and a normal level of ego. By understanding the relationships of pride, ego, and self-image leaders and workers in the normal work environment may be better prepared to avoid normal conflict that results from vagueness of these concepts, and to create a higher level of self-image for all members of their workplaces.

Pride, ego, and self-image are integrated and linked by the forces of relativity, significance, and quantity. Self-image is the result of these concepts and forces, not a force or a trait that evolves naturally. A person cannot have a good self-image unless that person balances pride and ego in situations that are relative to the accomplishments that developed that pride; and in situations where one's ego keeps the significance of those accomplishments in proper perspective.

Pride and ego are sometimes restricted by a perceived quantity factor. In many workplaces, as well as in general society, one's accomplishments will not be recognized by other people to make their accomplishments seem more significant. This suggests that some think there's only a limited quantity of pride of accomplishment, and they don't want to lose their share. Realistically, the amount of pride is limited only by one's imagination; and imagination is an endless resource.

Recognizing another's accomplishments to reinforce pride doesn't detract from another person's level or capacity for personal accomplishment. This reluctance to recognize accomplishment and achievement by other people is another interpersonal relationship that generates conflict in an organization. Let's consider an example:

Harry was a driver for a local delivery company in a large city. There were nine other full-time drivers for this company. The company was contracted to make deliveries for other servicing organizations; which included office supplies, office equipment, automobile parts, and any miscellaneous small items that didn't require special lifting equipment. The office was centrally located so that all parts of the city could be serviced quickly and easily. Ordinarily, it took about an hour to drive from one side of the city to the other. The central location of the office permitted drivers to arrive at the most distant location in about half an hour. The routine average for each driver was about twenty stops each day.

Clifton was Harry's supervisor. Clifton had weekly meetings with the drivers to encourage them to increase their delivery times so they could make at least two or three more pick-up and delivery stops each day. As many supervisors often suggest, Clifton suggested that they continue to improve themselves by learning to present a better customer service attitude, and even by trying to improve their education. Clifton told them that, "Any improvements that you make in yourself will not only improve the quality of our company, it will also increase your opportunities for advancement and promotion." He further emphasized that, "The closer we work together, the better it will be for all of us."

Harry, a young and enthusiastic worker who had been out of high school only a year, decided to try Harry's suggestions. He determined he would increase his delivery stops to at least an average of twenty-five, which he knew that he could do easily, anyway. Most of the drivers, including Harry, had planned to do an average of only twenty stops because that was all the company had ever really expected. There was no practical reason to do more. He also decided to begin a course in college. He enrolled in an English course to, hopefully, improve his communications skills.

Harry immediately increased his delivery stop average to twenty-seven a day. He could have increased it to over thirty, but he didn't want to create problems for other drivers who were still averaging only twenty a day. At the end of six weeks he also made a B on his first test in his English class. He was proud of these accomplishments. He was sure that Clifton would also be happy with these results, since it was Clifton's suggestion that this was the way to really increase career opportunities.

When Harry saw Clifton, the day after he had received his test grade, he told Clifton, "Boss, have you noticed; I raised my stop average to twenty-seven? Not only that, I also made a B on my first test in my English class. I hope I can continue making those good grades."

Clifton replied, "Well, everybody should be doing more than twenty-seven stops, and I hope you're not spending too much time studying to concentrate on your real work."

Harry continued to average around twenty-five stops on his delivery schedule. He also continued to take more college classes, since he finished the English class with a good grade. However, Harry didn't continue to trust Clifton or to openly communicate with him. He talked to Clifton only when a specific business topic had to be discussed. He lost his confidence that his supervisor, Clifton, would be fair and recognize the importance of the achievements that he had said were important. A gap was created in effective communications because Clifton refused to recognize Harry's achievements.

We can only guess the motive that caused Clifton to refuse to give Harry that recognition. Could it have been jealousy, oversight, lack of concern, or demonstration of poor leadership? Regardless of the reason, the result was restricted communications and distrust by Harry, which in most ordinary cases usually invite conflict into the relationship.

A simple, "That's great! Let me know if I can do anything to help you," by Clifton, would have created a productive and harmonious relationship. Is that not the purpose for leaders?

In this example, Harry was asking his supervisor for a

confirmation of his good self-image. Harry had developed pride in his accomplishments, and his ego had kept his bragging of those accomplishments within a socially acceptable level. Clifton's refusal to offer that confirmation to Harry's self-image made Harry question himself; and to question the validity and the purpose for his self-development efforts.

This example doesn't describe an unusual event. Much conflict is created in a work environment when members of that environment refuse to confirm and acknowledge another member's source of high self-image.

Resistance to Change

"Change! Change! Change! Why are they always changing things? I just learned how to do my job and now they want me to do it another way." This statement is a common complaint in most normal work environments. Often this complaint becomes so strong and so ingrained into the work environment that it generates endless conflict.

Change is an uncomfortable and often inconvenient fact of life. Resistance to change applies to leaders as well as workers, but it usually has a greater negative influence upon workers.

A person must face change if that person expects to live peacefully with himself or herself, and to continue to grow intellectually. In most cases one has no choice. Either a situation changes, which means one must change to fit into that environment, or procedures change, which one is instructed to follow. Those who are prepared to accept changes in their work environments are better prepared to progress in their careers. To accept change means they are open-minded, accommodating, and have confidence in themselves and other members of the workplace who generate those changes. Normal acceptance of change permits a harmonious environment in the workplace.

Those who resist change do injustice to themselves. When

changes are planned they are almost always enforced. They are planned, and they will be carried out. Those who resist demonstrate lack of self-confidence, trust, cooperation, self-discipline and conceptual understanding. Those who resist changes too vigorously eventually create such conflict that they disqualify themselves from promotions and other career opportunities.

Conditions and procedures always change. In the work environment changes are necessary for many reasons. Often one might become frustrated by changes, for that person might not know the reasons for those changes. The following identifies some of the common reasons for changes:

Changing Equipment and Technology

Business constantly competes, trying to produce a less expensive product, a higher quality product, a more functional product, or a more visible product. Any change in technology or improvement in production equipment to make those items means that a rapid conversion must be made to implement those processes to stay competitive in the market place. Failure to remain competitive in either price or quality of a product would cause a company to fail. A company constantly must change to exist.

Changing Product or Service Emphasis

To remain market competitive, a company must also change emphasis or areas of concentration on some of their products or services. For example, in times of prosperity a company that makes washing powder might concentrate on improved or eye-appealing packaging. During times of economic depression that same company might concentrate on reduced cost and economical packaging. A company might also change its emphasis from production to quicker service. A company can change its emphasis regarding economic classes and geographical marketing areas and strategies. Any imaginable reason can be used for marketing emphasis which will result in changes in the workplace.

Changing Leadership

Any change in leadership, at any level, could cause changes that affect a person at his or her job. Leaders are as different as other people in a work environment. They view their jobs and the environment around them in their own unique ways. No two leaders have the same perceptions to permit the job requirements to be identical. Consequently, something will always change when leadership changes.

Initially upon a leadership change, changes will usually be personnel policies and administration. Other changes will then be dictated by the leadership style and emphasis of the new leader. A leader who delegates well and motivates well will concentrate on general policies and results. A leader who cannot delegate effectively will routinely concentrate on specific details and procedures.

Changing Organizational Structure

Organizational structure changes also cause policy or procedural changes. This means that different people are in different jobs at various levels of the organization. Again, since different people are in those positions, the perceptions of their tasks and duties will be different. Those changed perceptions in the organizational structure might also result in changes in the work environment. That environment will probably be tense and apprehensive until everyone in the new organizational structure learns the requirements of his or her position, and how each job is associated with, and interacts to, other jobs and functions.

Trial and Error Actions

Frequent changes in the same area, or of the same function, are usually the result of trying to solve a problem by using the trail and error method. If one procedure or method doesn't solve a problem, another procedure is tried. This is called trial and error.

Trial and error is an acceptable method to solve some problems. This method would most probably be used in an area that's self-contained, where the function doesn't overlap or interact with another function that would cause additional coordination problems. Trial and error changes can be expected in a new office, or a newly established work environment, where historical alternatives aren't available to guide present actions.

Although changes are to improve conditions or to correct problems; sometimes changes have adverse affects upon direct workers, those who must change their personal procedures and methods. Adverse affects are exhibited by stress and anxiety. Stress might become apparent through several indicators. Some of these indicators include the following:

Bad attitudes. They might be disturbed and upset because the thing or the procedure that they know has been taken away from them. They have developed and refined the current procedure and it belongs to them. It's something that they personally own, and to change it isn't fair, according to their opinions.

Discomfort. The members have accepted methods and procedures that allow familiarity, like old friends. Any change reduces that comfort level - friends are lost.

Uncertainty. Only the most confident members of an organization will rush into a change without fear. Normally, however, a conscientious member will move into a change slowly, so that he or she will avoid mistakes. Even a formal retraining program can be stressful at a time of change, since there's an implied graded environment.

For example, a person will wonder if he or she did well, average, or poorly in the training environment. Any person who lacks confidence might even think this is an opportunity and a good reason for him or her to be replaced by someone who already knows the new procedure, or who can learn the new procedure more quickly.

Normal Reactions to Changes

There are two normal and predictable reactions to changes. One is supportive. The other is non-supportive. Naturally, the supportive reaction enhances workplace harmony; the non-supportive reactions ordinarily generate conflict.

The supportive reaction is the positive approach to change. The supportive member understands the reasons for change and gives his or her best efforts to make the change function effectively. That person's normal reaction is, "Why not! If the change will improve something, then I am the best person to make it work."

The non-supportive reaction is the negative approach to change that ordinarily generates workplace conflict. There are three statements that represent normal attempts to resist changes. They are:

"I can't do it that way."

"I've tried it that way before."

"It won't work."

These statements are counter-productive, and usually result not only in conflict but also in embarrassment for the person who says them. Changes are usually given enough forethought, or practice with a model, to insure they will result in the desired improvement.

One should expect and accept changes positively. Change can

be fun, and if nothing else, reduces boredom. A conscientious workplace member should understand that: *The winds of change can carry someone upward, or, the winds of change can blow someone away.*

A person who cannot accept changes in an organization will create two negative conditions. First, that person will contribute to the normal disharmony that ordinarily exists in an organization to create conflict. Secondly, that person will mark himself or herself as one who's not adaptable, and therefore not worthy or eligible for increased opportunities in that organization.

Summary

These values, beliefs, ideas, and judgements by members of an organization are fundamental parts of the individualism of each member. These personal traits are more universally inclusive than merely in the workplace. These are traits developed, encouraged, and reinforced through general social and cultural interaction. They are brought into the workplace to create harmony or conflict.

Consequently, an inordinate amount of focused training would be required for that training to have any affect or influence on those fundamental and individual traits. Most likely, even the most focused training to change the undesirable negative extremes of these personal traits would only subdue the outer expressions of those individualities, but would not change or influence those fundamental individual feelings.

All members of a work environment, including senior leaders, middle leaders, and workers, contribute their fundamental value judgements and traits to their work environments. These contributions basically express *who they think they are* not necessarily *who they really are* and what they can contribute to the productivity process. These trait influences relate to consideration of *self* and not to the mission or the task to be performed.

Formal training to control the extreme negatives of these trait conflicts historically has been in two forms:

Leadership and Management. This form includes management and leadership training and charm schools. Charm schools are used to teach leaders how to interact more effectively with their subordinates. Leaders who exhibit these negative traits are considered lacking only in training and development. Those negative traits aren't considered fundamental values in leaders.

Disciplinary Actions: for workers and subordinates. This training is usually in the form of threatening, counseling, and formal disciplinary actions against the offending person. Subordinates who exhibit negative traits are often considered unintelligent and selfish trouble-makers or incompetents; both conditions created by their weak fundamental values.

These last three chapters have identified the basic components that create the zone of conflict in a work environment. Chapter Three identified major leadership considerations that contribute to conflict. Chapter Four identified major worker considerations that also contribute to workplace conflict. This chapter analyzed some of the major traits and values that all members of a work environment contribute to the conflict zone.

Managing The Conflict Zone

6

MISTAKES: HARMONY OR CONFLICT

Many leaders and workers fail to reach their highest potential for productivity and harmony in the work environment for they fear that some decisions and some actions will cause them to make mistakes. Some people, leaders as well as workers, fear mistakes from a lifetime learning process, a basis not directly related to the work environment. Others fear making mistakes as a consequence of their general lack of self-confidence. Still others fear mistakes due to apprehension related to their superiors. This apprehension may have a factual base, or it may be based upon one's imagination.

Mistakes are always feared, at least to some degree. Sometimes a small level of fear, anxiety, may be helpful in increasing one's level of concentration to resolve problems. On the other hand, however, a higher level of fear will cause actions or inactions in a work environment that may naturally produce conflict that inhibits productivity.

Although some fear of mistakes will always be present, that fear should be in the form of striving for excellence. It shouldn't be in forms of obstacles and conflicts.

All members of a work environment, including leaders and workers, should understand the effects caused by fear of mistakes and the role that those effects have upon the achievements and failures of their environments. Ordinarily, members in a workplace who understand how to deal with mistakes will have a workplace that's cooperative, courteous, and productive. Members in a workplace who don't understand the significance of mistakes will have a workplace that's typically fearful, defensive, uncooperative, and riddled with conflict. The implications of mistakes will be analyzed further to provide this understanding.

Understanding Mistakes

Making mistakes is a common trait of humanity. Anyone who believes he or she never makes mistakes is out of step with reality, and might even have a psychological problem. Mistakes will be discussed here. To ignore this discussion would probably be a mistake.

Mistakes are generally considered negative, and something that one would always want to avoid. This discussion is to explain that mistakes are sometimes logical and shouldn't always be regarded as failure. They should be positively regarded as a level of success, if those mistakes can be used to eliminate conflict by analyzing and solving real problems.

There are three important variables of making decisions or taking actions that could result in that action being called a mistake. They are:

All necessary information is rarely available to insure a perfect decision, without some risk.

There's rarely only one correct decision to make, or only one way to do something.

There's always someone who knows how to do it better, after the fact.

Ordinarily, decisions are made casually, or actions are taken without one considering all the information or circumstances surrounding the question or task. People are more casual about their approach to an action or an event if they are more knowledgeable about the subject in their particular area of expertise. People do some things so many times they don't have to think about the why or how of doing them. They know that it's the right way because it's always been done that way.

Is it possible that a mistake is routinely made without it being recognized as a mistake? If something could be done better in another manner is it a mistake to continue the present method? Is a mistake really a mistake or simply a selection of alternative choices, either of which could be categorized as a mistake, depending upon the results?

For an illustration, let's use the example of a football coach making a decision:

A coach is involved in a big game. The score is tied, and every inch counts. The coach calls for a play that requires the running back to carry the football straight up the middle. As the play begins, the quarterback hands the ball to the running back, charging through the middle of the line. The coach observes that, at the same time, the left end has gone down field twenty yards, and is all alone. The coach is also surprised to see the defensive line on the right side, trip themselves and fall. The running back manages to push his way, gropingly, for five yards.

Now, for the question: did the coach make a mistake? If the coach had called a pass play, the left end would probably have scored the winning touchdown. If the coach had called a play to run around the right side of the line, the team would easily have made ten to twenty yards, and maybe even a touchdown.

Is that failure to score a touchdown really a mistake? Before this question can be answered, those three important variables that influence mistakes should be analyzed: Was all the information available before the coach made the decision? Was there only one correct decision that could have been made? Could the decision be made better by someone else, now?

Obviously, all the information wasn't available before the coach called that play; before he had to make that decision. The coach didn't know that backfield defenders would not be watching the left end, so that the end would be wide open to catch a pass. The coach didn't have the information that the defensive line on the right side would fall down, so a runner going wide would make a long gain.

What would have been the correct decision? Was there only one perfectly correct decision? After knowing these facts, the opposing coach would probably tell that coach that he made a 'big mistake' by not throwing a pass to the left end. That opposing coach is really a genius.

Did that coach make a mistake by calling that running play up the middle? Of course not. That coach had observed the middle of the line seemed to be the opponent's weakest defensive area. And, the offensive team did advance the ball five yards closer to the goal line.

No one will ever know, for sure, if that team quarterback would have made an accurate pass to the end, if the left end would have caught the football, or even if the left end would have fallen. No one will ever know if the handoff to a running back going around the right side would have been fumbled, or if the running back going to the right side would have accelerated too fast, and lost his footing. Again, considering those three variables that influence judgement on decisions, the coach made the correct decision. He didn't make a mistake.

Mistakes: Two Approaches

There are also two approaches that may be taken, regarding mistakes. One is the learning approach. The other is the attention approach.

Learning Mistakes

The learning approach to mistakes makes the assumption that some mistakes are caused by lack of information, lack of practice or lack of experience. These mistakes are expected from a new employee, or an employee entering into a new environment. It's expected that some mistakes will occur under these situations. Except in technical fields, or unusual situations, systems allow a small tolerance for mistakes or audit procedures are in place to make corrections. The learning approach also assumes that with normal practice and experience, mistakes should decrease to an acceptable level, or to an acceptable frequency of occurrence. If a person is at least average in mental capacity and diligence, that person will be permitted some errors or mistakes on a new job or in a new situation.

Each mistake, however, should be a learning experience that one analyzes to prevent other mistakes. Under the learning approach to mistakes, a person is permitted learning mistakes.

Those mistakes, however, should decrease in severity and frequency. If not, normal conflict will result.

One should understand those mistakes to insure all conditions and situations surrounding those mistakes are known and analyzed. Trying to hide part of the circumstance causing those mistakes could result in continuing mistakes, or even worse mistakes. One should also be sincere when evaluating his or her situation. That person should show a genuine concern, so that those leaders who are responsible can be comfortable with the worker's effort and level of understanding.

Attention Mistakes

The attention approach to mistakes can be divided into three categories, which are:

Ability. Mistakes are often caused by the lack of mental capacity or manual dexterity that will not allow one to perform required functions, with only normal severity or frequency of errors. This analysis is not to judge a person's intelligence or educational level. This discussion merely considers a person's qualifications and compatibility with a specific job, function, or requirement. If a person cannot perform the job without continuous or repetitive mistakes, then it's an attention mistake not to make personnel or job adjustments.

Some people are not qualified or competent for some jobs. It would be a mistake if the leader didn't make an adjustment, even if the worker must be terminated. It would be a mistake for the worker, for continued mistakes would erode that worker's self-confidence and esteem. This would not only create more workplace conflict, it could also have a negative effect upon any future efforts of that person. That worker should find a new job that provides comfort and potential for that worker's capabilities.

Boredom. Sometimes a job is so uninspiring and boring a worker cannot maintain necessary concentration. This is an area into which many employees become trapped. One cause is knowing the function so well that the job is almost an automatic and unconscious response. Another common cause is comparing one's job to other jobs, which makes that job seem less important.

Some people have these thoughts about their jobs. Fortunately, this is the attention area easiest to correct. It's also the area that permits a worker to seek more accomplishments and feelings of achievement.

One might ask, "How can I reach higher accomplishments if I'm bored on the job?" The answer is simple. One can set 'game' job goals for himself or herself. Or, one can see how quickly he or she can complete the job, so that he or she can learn something new at someone else's job.

For example, suppose a worker is required to drill

five-hundred widgets a day. Suppose, also, that worker is so qualified at that job he or she must reduce speed to make five hundred widgets last all day. *Is there anything more boring than trying to make a small job last longer?*

Since that worker is so proficient at his or her job, why shouldn't that person try to reach new records at that job? Why shouldn't he or she set a goal of seven hundred widgets? Then, why shouldn't that person reach for eight hundred. Probably no one's ever done a thousand widgets.

When the worker is finished with those widgets, why shouldn't he or she volunteer to help Joe or Sam with their jobs? They seem always to be behind with their work, and need help. Maybe that person could even help Joe or Sam learn to make their jobs more fun and exciting. What could be more inventive and ingenious than to make a boring job fun and exciting?

Naturally, a certain degree of pride, and maybe even due recognition, would be added bonuses for that imaginative person. Of course this person must understand the fundamentals of good employeeship, or be determined to become successful by another unknown method.

Sabotage or carelessness. The most inexcusable attention mistake is that caused by sabotage or extreme carelessness. Ordinarily, one might not consider the results of sabotage as a mistake. However, the results of sabotage would be discovered as a mistake. A mistake made by carelessness would produce the same results. Therefore, the results produced by the mistakes of sabotage or extreme carelessness are the same. These are the negative mistakes that shouldn't be tolerated. These are the mistakes that show no probability of improvement in those areas of concern, without an attitude change from those workers.

Why would anyone intentionally or carelessly cause an error or mistake, especially when it could cause that person to lose his or her job, or some other severe penalty? These acts usually result from anger, frustration, or revenge. These emotions ordinarily result from workplace conflict, and tend to create even more workplace conflict. It's not uncommon in a workplace to hear someone say, "I don't care what happens - I'm going to get back at him. I'm going to get even." "They don't appreciate what I do." Or, "Who cares? This place is run by a bunch of jerks." These comments are symptomatic of an attitude or personality problem. The attitude problem might result from a direct job situation, or the problem might have nothing to do with that job.

A person with this attitude should immediately correct himself or herself. If not, management should take necessary management action. If a destructive attitude isn't corrected it can only grow. This attitude can even affect people who know the difference between what's right and wrong, fair and unfair, and rational or irrational.

A person who develops this thought process, that which causes carelessness, must correct that condition. That is, assuming of course, that extreme carelessness isn't one's normal nature. This condition of extraordinary carelessness would indicate a personality disorder or emotional stress that one must recognize and resolve.

How should one control negative and destructive emotions in the workplace? First, that person should pause and take some deep breaths to relax. One might be surprised to learn that stress may cause one's breathing apparatus to restrict so that he or she cannot breath properly. That person should breath a few deep breaths to relax those tightened muscles and diaphragm to allow his or her normal breathing rhythm to return. Then that person should ask himself or herself, "What caused me to be so tense?" The worker, or leader, should identify the problem and not ignore or avoid it. A situation is there to cause problems unless one understands the situation and deals with it. The source, or cause, of the problem might be someone else or it might be only that person's imagination or apprehension.

Once the problem is identified there are correction processes: The person may rationalize the problem by suggesting to himself or herself that the action should not have happened, and it's really not as serious as it seems. The person may use the problem solving technique to find a   reasonable solution. Or, that person may concentrate on some pleasant thoughts, events, or plans to buffer or ameliorate some of the stress.

In any event, the person shouldn't concentrate on just forgetting the problem. That will cause the condition to have added reinforcement. Continued negative mistakes would eventually result in more conflict that might cause a person to lose his or her self-esteem, confidence and job.

Risk of Making Mistakes

There's another important consideration of mistakes. This concerns risk. Nothing significant or important is seldom achieved or accomplished without some risk.

There's usually no great probability of repeating those learning mistakes when one does the same things, in the same way, repetitiously. One knows how to do those things, and one knows what the usual result will be. There's little risk involved, after a person does something repetitively and routinely. On the other hand, neither are there any great expectations for improvement, enhancement, or increased success. To make those advances, something must be done differently.

Doing something differently, or doing something else, increases the possibility of mistakes. There's increased risk involved. Therefore, to make improvements a person must occasionally take risks. When one takes risks, that person might make mistakes. When one recognizes these mistakes, he or she makes adjustments and continues with improvements. Most major improvements require some mistakes that contribute to the learning process.

Summary

There are learning mistakes and bad mistakes. The learning mistakes are those that occur as lessons while trying to improve or change something. These mistakes should routinely decrease. The result should be increased efficiency and performance.

The bad or negative mistakes are caused by situations or circumstances that require specific attention to correct. They aren't lessons. They are obstacles or barriers. To maintain efficiency, effectiveness, a good job atmosphere and normalcy, either the negative mistakes or their source should be quickly eliminated or adjusted. If not, conflict will remain a dominant part of that work environment.

These first six chapters identify sources, forces and influences that create or perpetuate conflict in a normal work environment. The remaining chapters are designed to show how these conflicts are related, and how to develop relationships in organizations that will reduce the negative effects of those conflicts. A descriptive model of the basic conflict zone will be analyzed in the next chapter.

7

THE CONFLICT ZONE

An understanding of the conflict zone would be more difficult without the background information in the first six chapters. By sorting and synthesizing the information contained in those chapters, a model may be constructed that gives a visual presentation of the conflict that routinely limits and restricts effective productivity in most business and industrial organizations. The purpose of this chapter is to create that clear model.

To make the visual model more meaningful, let's briefly review the first six chapters to see how each chapter is an important and integral part of the conflict puzzle. By piecing that information together, a visual model may be created:

Chapter One - Conflict Dimensions. This chapter explained that conflict may occur at any level of an organization; and, that conflict at any level creates conflict at all other levels.

Chapter Two - Conflict Sources. This chapter identified universal ideas, values and feelings among people that are important enough to create disharmony in an organization.

Chapter Three - Leadership Forces. This chapter identified specific and unique concerns and pressures on leaders that force them to function from a traditional leadership perspective.

Chapter Four - Employeeship Forces. This chapter introduced a new concept into the work environment; that of employeeship. Employeeship was briefly described as a concept that requires workers to be responsible for their personal career planning as well as for their own internal motivation. This chapter also gave specific employeeship concerns from a worker's perspective.

Chapter Five - Other Conflict Forces. This chapter identified general forces and influences that affect people's actions and decisions, whether they are leaders or workers. These are personality and value factors that aren't normally influenced significantly by training. These are those traits that are part of one's nature.

Chapter Six - Mistakes. This analysis demonstrated how mistakes contribute to distrust and conflict. It also revealed that some mistakes may be used for a positive purpose.

Why is a conflict model necessary?

A conflict model is necessary for two reasons. The first is merely to acknowledge that conflict does, in fact, exist in a work environment; and to understand conflict may be initiated by any member of that environment. The second reason is to establish, visually, a basis for reducing or removing conflict from the work environment to allow increased harmony and productivity.

Productivity is the most important result, from a practical and economic consideration. From a company's perspective, and from the perspective of the economic well-being of a society, productivity is the basis for survival and growth. Without productivity in a society nothing else in that society will sustain itself and grow. Increased productivity is also necessary for individuals, for without productivity new jobs and opportunities cannot be created to allow them a source of meaningful work and personal growth.

Workplace harmony is also important for it increases the quality of life; physical, mental and psychological, for every member in that workplace. It's possible for a workplace to be productive without having harmonious relationships in that environment; however, the depreciation and damage to future human potential are usually not considered as losses in that tentative productivity gain. Disharmony and excess conflict in a work environment not only tend to destroy one's interest and motivation in that workplace, those conditions may also affect a person's private life and overall career potential as well.

Basis of the conflict zone

The conflict zone is formed by values, opinions, and interests of leaders and workers. Perceptions of each other's interests also play a major role in forming that conflict zone. The following influences and interests are major causes of conflict and disharmony:

- The leader's responsibility for productivity
- The leader's approach to leadership
- The leader's personality
- The leader's personal career concerns
- The worker's expectations
- The worker's skill and training
- The worker's cultural values
- The worker's employeeship concerns
- The worker's personality

These things are important for there are no standards or models to help determine the best or most appropriate traits and characteristics. For example, there's no perfect leader personality or worker personality that fits into every situation to produce the same results. Even if a perfect personality model could be described, most probably that perfect personality wouldn't fit on other people. Personality is important but it must be considered along with its environment and the particular situation.

A leader's approach to leadership is also important, but that also depends upon each situation. One cannot say with certainty that the *Theory Y* leadership approach, explained in previous chapters, is better for harmony and productivity than is the *Theory X* approach. Perhaps the Theory Y approach wouldn't be better, assuming that leader doesn't have natural Theory Y tendencies; and, also assuming workers are more comfortable with a Theory X leader; as in the case of some workers from culturally deprived backgrounds.

Although all those influences and interests shown above have some impact upon productivity and conflict, the all-inclusive factors most dominant and influential are: leadership theories; leadership style, as a leadership responsibility; and level of employeeship, as a worker responsibility. These all-inclusive factors include those individual factors plus other less identifiable motivations and variables.

Leadership theories and leadership styles are explained in Chapter Three, and employeeship is described in Chapter Four. An analysis of their relationships will be made here, however, to show their direct contributions to the conflict zone.

Leadership Theories

The three leadership theories analyzed in Chapter Three included: Blake and Mouton's *Managerial Grid*, Tannenbaum and Schmidt's *Continuum of Leadership Theory*, and *The Two-Dimensional Theory*. Although those three theories are somewhat different in terms and in presentation they, nevertheless, have several mutual implications. These implications refer to normal conflict that exists in workplaces. That conflict is the consideration of productivity factors versus the human relations and human need factors. The common assumptions of these three theories are:

- The leader, or manager, is the only one who's responsible for productivity.

- The leader has the ability to make a clear choice between concerns of productivity and concerns for people.

- The leader is not restricted or pressured by superiors or personal problems in the decision process.

- Subordinates aren't active participants in resolving or increasing the overall workplace conflict. They are considered as tools or 'bystanders.'

In summary, these three theories imply that workplace conflict is recognized. However, that conflict recognized by these theories is productivity concerns versus people concerns. These theories don't consider that extenuating circumstances such as personality, cultural expectations and leadership hierarchies routinely prevent leaders from making those decisions. Those decisions are often dictated by higher authority, they're often required by the actions of subordinates and they're sometimes made by habit.

Nevertheless, these three theories, in their similarity, confirm there are three considerations in the workplace that guide leadership actions. These three considerations are: leaders, subordinates and the overall situation. The relationships between and among these three variables determine the level of conflict in a work environment.

Leadership Styles

Every leader has a certain style that he or she uses to perform the tasks that he or she interprets as part of the leadership function. A leadership style objectively cannot be identified as good or bad, for that would require a judgmental evaluation of an unknown factor. That determination would also depend upon the position of the person making that judgement.

For example, a subordinate might dislike his or her boss regardless of the boss's leadership style. In this case, the boss would be determined by that subordinate to be a 'bad' leader regardless of that leader's style. Would that subordinate dislike a 'good' leader? In this case that determination would be made more from personality than from leadership ability.

On the other hand, a leader's superior might take a different approach to the determination of the leader's ability. Most likely the superior's determination would be influenced more by productivity and profit than by the homogeneous compatibility of people in that leader's department. If the leader's performing effectively to protect the profits and job security of the superior leader, then that subordinate leader is, in fact, a good leader.

These two examples give the basis for the determination of a 'good' leader. Those two bases of determination are the position of the evaluator and the personal interests of the evaluator. A leader who doesn't comply with or fulfill the personal interests of the evaluator will most likely be determined a 'bad' leader by the person making that determination.

This lack of objectivity, or the absence of a reasonable model of a good leader, eliminates this concept as a fair method of categorizing leadership styles. This presents a frustrating dilemma, however, in the compatibility of an organization, for the conflict zone develops largely from this biased determination of a leader's character. Some major factors in determining the quality of leadership style include:

Autocratic Leadership. Autocratic leadership is the style that's generally regarded as the 'bad' leadership style. This conclusion, however, is made only under certain conditions. One of those conditions is that the larger organization, or the immediate superior leader, understands and prefers the human relations leadership style. Another condition is that workers in the organization are skilled and expect a leadership style that respects their middle-class values. In this case, workers would anticipate enough freedom for personal growth and development in their careers. Another significant condition is the accepted level and anticipation of leadership standards in the local society. Some geographical areas have different ideas and concepts of leadership styles.

Human Relations Leadership. The human relations leadership style is generally regarded as the 'good' leadership style. This style is less directive in nature and considers the needs and feelings of workers as well as the needs of the job and productivity. There are times and conditions, however, when the human relations style isn't considered a good style. This would occur when the organizational culture is targeted primarily on scientific methods of productivity. Highly structured organizations don't take human factors into their engineering, work design and process planning.

Another situation that would make the effectiveness of the human relations leadership style questionable concerns leadership of culturally deprived workers who have no history or role models of workplace success. Ordinarily the lower cultures lack the confidence, the skills and the training to work independently, without close guidance and supervision. Those workers would consider a leader who's not interested enough to tell them what to do as a bad leader.

The Laissez-Faire Style. Laissez-Faire leadership is an abdication of leadership. The leader who practices this style is present but not functioning as a leader. Although it might seem improbable, this leadership condition does occur. Its causes are usually based on fear or disinterest.

For example, a leader who fears his or her immediate superior might be hesitant to make decisions that the superior might dislike. Another example is when a leader doesn't want to 'rock the boat' for he or she is nearing retirement, and doesn't want to do anything that would jeopardize that retirement. It must also be recognized that many leaders simply aren't suited for leadership, or for the special functional responsibilities that they are to lead. Finally, some leaders prefer to work than to lead others in accomplishing that work. These are all bases of laissez-faire leadership.

Is laissez-faire leadership a good style or a bad style? As with the other leadership styles, it depends upon the evaluator and the situation. A superior leader might be glad to see the laissez-faire leader do nothing, for it might fit the style of the superior leader. On the other hand, an effective superior leader wouldn't tolerate this do-nothing style. Skilled and self-directed workers might enjoy the challenge of protecting the boss who doesn't hassle them, until organizational pressure is created by low productivity or inefficiency. Lazy and less-inspired workers would probably resent a lazy boss.

A perfect leadership style that will routinely and automatically reduce or eliminate conflict in the workplace doesn't exist. Neither can a style be labeled good or bad, since there are too many variables to leave either style unchallenged. These styles, however, should be identified and recognized for they are major contributors to normal workplace conflict.

Employeeship

The leadership theories and leadership styles, identified above, don't consider employeeship. Employeeship must be an important factor to any leadership condition or question, since employeeship must be considered as contributing to most of the overall productivity effort.

Leadership efforts toward productivity and human concerns

should comprise no more than an equal share of the total workplace and productivity effort. For example, if there are five people in a workplace, with one as the leader, that leader's share of the productivity process would be no more than twenty percent. If a workplace had ten people and one is the leader, that leader's share of the process should be no more than ten percent. That ten percent would include planning, organizing, providing essentials, evaluating and training.

Actual task functions should be accomplished by workers performing employeeship. That employeeship would include the full authority and the responsibility to make job and task decisions, from clearly established delegations, within their work assignments. The essentials of employeeship are discussed in Chapter Four.

The Leadership-Employeeship Factor

The zone of conflict develops when leadership theories, leadership styles and employeeship within a workplace aren't harmonious or compatible, or when either leaders or workers fail to perform their functions. Conflict may be initiated, or caused, by leaders or workers; and deeper conflict may even result from further actions and reactions by the other party.

Leaders must recognize that actual work and those routine decisions to perform that work must ordinarily be performed by those workers who are hired for that work. Once workers are trained for their jobs and have the tools to do those jobs leaders must become more facilitative and less directive in those standard procedures. Productivity effort must be performed by workers.

Workers must understand that good employeeship is the purpose for their existence. Leaders must acknowledge their obligation to support and assist those workers to reach productivity goals.

With these acknowledgments, it should be mutually

understood that any productivity effort by the leader above an equally shared amount would be considered as an acquiescence factor by that worker; or as an encroachment by the leader. This includes the understanding that the workload remains constant, and other productivity factors remain unchanged - or that adjustments are made to account for these additional factors.

If a leader must increase his or her efforts to encourage or demand increased employeeship from workers, that extra effort would be caused by employee acquiescence. On the other hand, if the leader increases his or her involvement voluntarily, that increase would be leadership encroachment.

The three graphics on the next page illustrate this acquiescence and encroachment concept. For this example, a workforce of ten people including the leader will be considered. The leader's share would be ten percent of the productivity process.

Figure 1

Normal

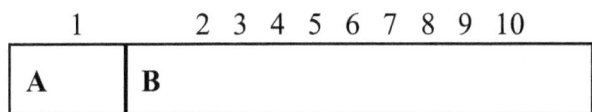

Figure 2

Acquiescence

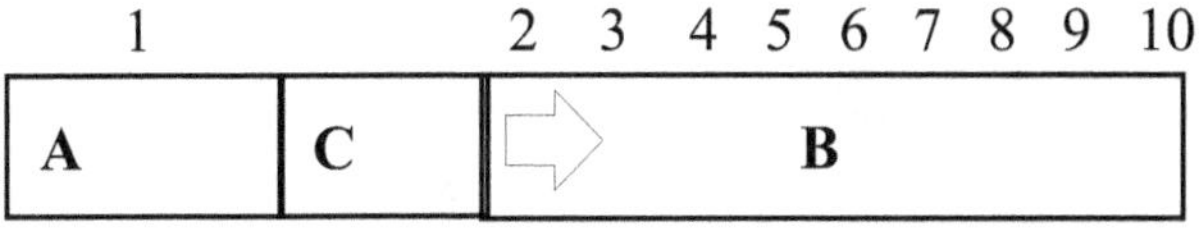

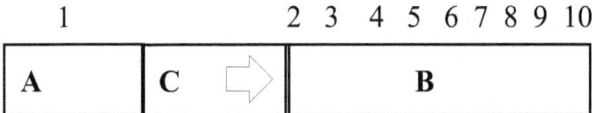

Figure 3

Encroachment

In these graphics, A is the leadership zone of normal activity. A leader using either leadership style that's compatible with that work environment would perform normal functions expected of that leader without reducing workers' opportunities for achievement, satisfaction, esteem and meaningful work. The employeeship zone includes the area identified as B. In this figure, workers would understand their duties, be skillfully trained, and would perform those duties without further close supervision and encouragement. **Figure 1** demonstrates that harmonious relationship between leadership and employeeship.

Figure 2 suggests employeeship has acquiesced by twenty percent, demonstrated by area C. This means workers haven't fulfilled their responsibilities and duties under the concept of employeeship. This demonstrates they are lazy, untrained, unmotivated, disinterested or intentionally plan not to cooperate with management in the productivity process.

Figure 3 shows leadership has encroached by thirty percent, also represented by area C. This case represents a directive leader who likes to do the work in the productivity process, or who doesn't trust those workers to work effectively.

Analysis of acquiescence and encroachment

The graphics represent the basic work environment conflict. That conflict is created by productivity versus people concerns; and it's further complicated by personalities of each individual. Figure 1 represents a workplace condition of natural productivity, mutual respect, and understanding of tasks, responsibilities and delegations. Subordinates understand and practice good employeeship. Leaders maintain a supportive relationship that includes removal of demotivators and obstacles for those subordinates. Probably a selfish and dominating personality wouldn't exist in this organization. Figure 2 identifies a work environment with demotivated, lazy, or unskilled workers. Effective employeeship is not maintained; consequently, area C must be filled by increased leadership to lead that employeeship back to full effectiveness. This necessary entry into area C by leadership is a condition that generates conflict, for it's not the natural order. The degree of conflict is usually determined by the quality of that leader. However, it might also be influenced by ulterior motives of those employees, if that deficiency is caused by factors other than weak training.

Figure 3 suggests an inexperienced and untrained leader or an autocratic leader. An untrained leader, sincere in the learning process, will eventually remove himself or herself from the encroached area. The autocratic leader, on the other hand, cannot function without maintaining a position inside that encroached zone. This permanent encroachment by leadership doesn't allow workers to exhibit full employeeship. Without full employeeship, workers are not permitted to reach the level of workplace achievement that's essential for them to attain personal success goals. Without an opportunity for achievement, conflict arises.

The conflict zone in any work environment or in any productivity process negatively affects the operational capabilities of that environment. The larger the conflict zone, the less effective will be that organization. This ineffectiveness has a direct and negative impact upon individual workers, leaders, companies, and even a country.

Workers who create the conflict zone by their acquiescence of effective employeeship create more harm to themselves than to their leaders or their company. Their acquiescence may result from the following conditions:

- Lack of skill and confidence
- Laziness and lack of motivation
- Health or psychological problems
- Peer pressure

- Intentional revenge

From this list it's easily determined that conflict can occur naturally, as with the natural tendency toward laziness or a natural tendency for some to lack confidence. It may also be recognized that some workplace conflict is created by peer pressure to encourage workers toward goals not directly related to high productivity; and, from purposeful actions by some workers to make their boss 'look bad.' In either case, these workers aren't fulfilling employeeship responsibilities. By not fulfilling those responsibilities, those workers aren't completing the actions necessary to develop a rewarding and purposeful career that will give themselves a feeling of achievement and satisfaction. Under these conditions it will be impossible for these workers to ever reach goals they desire most: esteem, recognition, and self-respect.

Leaders also share in creating the conflict zone in the normal work environment. Although most rhetoric concerning lack of productivity is focused toward the inadequacies of modern-age workers, much of that rhetoric is really used by leaders to camouflage their own weaknesses, incompetence and inadequacies.

Leaders' contributions to the conflict zone, however, are different from those of workers. Leader encroachment, or acquiescence, ordinarily results from the following:

Use of the Theory X leadership approach

Untrained leaders

Cowardly or fearful leaders

leaders with low character traits

Leaders who are selfish and neglectful

Leaders who focus only on the work process

Leaders who should not be in leadership positions

These leader inadequacies suggest leader-induced conflict has two fundamental bases. These include the leader's personality, people skills, and the leader's concern for productivity at the exclusion of concern for people. It would be rare, indeed, for a leader to take any action that would intentionally be detrimental to the productivity process that he or she is charged to accomplish.

Summary

A zone of conflict exists in every organization whether that organization is a proprietorship, a partnership, or a corporation. The size, or the width, of that conflict zone determines the level of performance, compared to the organization's optimum capability.

For example, an organization with a ten percent zone of conflict might produce at ninety percent of its optimum capability. Its optimum capability might be only eighty percent of its maximum capability. In this example, the productivity level would be only seventy percent of that maximum capability.

According to management experts the zone of conflict must be significantly higher than ten percent, for their consensus is that most workers perform at approximately fifty percent of their capability. Is it possible that the zone of conflict could be as high as twenty-five to thirty percent? If the conflict zone is that high, who's to blame for the great loss of productivity that ultimately determines the success of individuals, companies and countries?

The purpose for the graphic, or the conflict model, above, is to present a visualization of the conflict zone so it may be presented as something substantive; not something that exists merely as a topic of casual conversation. The conflict zone clearly exists, and it clearly has identifiable causes.

Some causes are somewhat obvious, as in the case of worker acquiescence. When workers don't perform effective employeeship, that fact cannot be hidden for long. It becomes self-evident.

On the other hand, the conflict zone is also created, or generated, by other less obvious actions or influences. One of those major contributors is leadership encroachment. When a leader encroaches into those areas of productivity that should be performed by employeeship, that leader isolates workers from the higher benefits that workers hope to gain from their good employeeship: meaningful work, achievement, and recognition. If workers cannot feel they will earn these just rewards from dedicated effort, there's no reason to make that dedicated effort just so a selfish or autocratic leader can claim those rewards for himself or herself.

The zone of conflict may also be created by leadership acquiescence. In this case a leader abandons or abdicates true leadership responsibilities, or is basically untrained or incompetent. An unusual paradox may also occur during leadership acquiescence. If the workforce is highly skilled and dedicated, and strong positive peer leadership exists within that workforce, an emergent informal leader might assume leadership to maintain effective productivity. It's possible this paradox might explain why some weak or untrained leaders occasionally have better results in their organizations than highly trained more autocratic leaders.

Another influence also helps to generate and maintain workplace conflict. That concerns social and political restrictions. This influence will be discussed later.

8

GOALS OF HARMONY

The first six chapters of this book identified the dimensions, influences, and causes of conflict in the normal work environment. Chapter Seven assimilated the information given in the first six chapters into a clear model identified as the zone of conflict. This model now provides the clarity to recognize conflict in the workplace as a distinct character; and as such, something that can be controlled, or at least recognized and alleviated.

This action, however, requires more information and planning. That will be the purpose for the remaining chapters of this book, to provide that positive information to eliminate or to reduce conflict in the normal work environment.

The first step in any planning process is to understand goals. That's the purpose of this chapter.

Goal Expectations

It's an understatement to suggest that goals are the most important forces in advancement and development. This concept is as valid for individuals as it is for corporations or any other entity. As profound and as important as goals are to success, goals are the least understood, the least emphasized, and the least recognized force in a work environment that causes, or permits, most conflict. This concept is so important it must be emphasized:

143

The absence of clear and reasonable goals by individuals in an organization, and the lack of recognition of those absent goals by leaders, are the core foundations of most workplace conflict.

This idea will be examined to understand the importance and effects of goals as they relate to achievement, success, frustration, and despair.

Goals often are defeated by routine expectations. Often, goals aren't clearly formed in a work environment for leaders expect certain actions from workers and workers expect certain actions from leaders. Although these actions may not be discussed or planned, they are normally assumed.

In some instances these workplace assumptions are so strong they may even be discussed as a matter of fact. The following two examples illustrate typical assumptions by leaders and workers that set the stage for conflict in the workplace. The two examples also expose the fundamental conflict.

Leader Assumptions

Leaders assume workers get a job for reasonable purposes; to earn money for financial security. When a worker applies for a job, this is ordinarily the overriding purpose. During the hiring interview process, the prospective worker promises to work hard and to be a loyal and dedicated employee as long as the pay is reasonable and fair.

In many cases at the time of initial hiring any pay is accepted as reasonable and fair. Since many leaders pride themselves on being great judges of honesty, integrity, and character, they assume they can choose the best candidate for the job based upon their judgement. Workers usually promise to remain loyal, dedicated and effective. Leaders tend to assume those candidates are telling the truth, since they are the judges of that truth.

At the time of that interview, both the leader and the worker candidate are assuming the truth. At that time, the potential worker is telling the truth, for that worker honestly plans to be a loyal and dedicated person for that company. The motivation at that time for the worker is an unfulfilled need for money for security and survival. This need overrides all other considerations the potential worker will certainly face in the future after that need has been fulfilled. At this time, the leader should assume the candidate for the job is telling the truth, for he or she is, based upon perceptions at that moment in time.

The leader's assumption is that the chosen worker will be diligent and effective simply by being chosen for the job. At this time also, most leaders have certain biases that lead them to choose a worker with characteristics that are perceived as good, for they are similar to those characteristics of the person making the selection.

Worker Assumptions

Workers apply for a job also with inherent assumptions. In a lower status job, a worker assumes that the job will only be a temporary job until he or she can find a real job. In higher status jobs, workers assume that the job will be an opportunity for normal career development. In either case, however, the potential worker must make the interviewer think that he or she really wants the job for a long term career. The assumption is that an applicant applies for a job as an entry level into a permanent career.

As a follow-up to this assumption that workers come into a job as an entry into a career, leaders routinely encourage those workers to "do a good job and there are plenty of opportunities for you to advance and have a good career in this company." Workers ordinarily assume leaders are in a position to know that information, so they assume that what the leader tells them must be true.

Based on this typical advice, workers believe the workplace they have chosen is their opportunity for financial and personal success. Workers assume that if they 'do a good job' the company will advance them financially and personally. They will become wealthy persons of high esteem by simply doing a good job for the company.

Customarily and traditionally, however, reality begins to rule in the work environment for the new worker, and the relationship with the leader. The new worker quickly learns he or she is simply a tool to be used by the company, as long as the company needs that worker as a tool. The new worker also assumed the leader would help him or her to become successful; and that leader will not even take time to carry on a normal conversation with the worker. Often, the only conversation the worker receives from the leader is criticism for laziness, inefficiency, stupidity, and too many mistakes.

The worker quickly learns, in about sixty to ninety days, that the leader is not going to do what the leader said he or she would do, by words or by innuendo, to help that worker become successful. The leader, coincidentally, notices the worker has become less attentive, less dedicated, and less effective than the worker appeared to be when that worker was hired into the company. The leader assumes another typical and unmotivated worker has been hired.

Goal Relationships

The definition of goals is a misunderstood and misused word concept in the work environment that causes much agony and conflict for leaders and workers. Before conflict in the workplace may be resolved, leaders and workers must understand the importance, the relationship, and the implications of goals. Both leaders and workers function under the illusion that company goals and workers' goals are compatible and identical, or at least they should be.

Nothing could be more inaccurate. This false assumption continues to create frustration, disharmony, and conflict in most work environments. This misconception doesn't allow effective leadership development or practical motivational concepts to encourage workers to work at a consistently productive level.

146

This false assumption is that workers' goals should be the same as company goals or that workers should adopt company goals as their own. This logical assumption is based on the idea that if the company continues to meet its goals workers will have more opportunities for increased pay and advancement in their careers. To leaders and managers this is only a logical conclusion, for those leaders and managers have adopted that concept since they feel they are part of the company. In fact, they are part of the ruling part of the organization until the organization decides to reorganize or down-size, and their positions are lost or downgraded.

Even naive workers soon learn that the concept that seems economically logical is really an illusion and a false promise. In most typical organizations, when that organization achieves its goals of profit and productivity, that increased profit is not ordinarily used to advance workers. It's ordinarily used for management bonuses and higher dividends to stockholders. Workers ordinarily receive the same pay increase they would have received regardless of company profit.

This concept alone, without additional support, suggests that goals of corporations aren't synonymous with goals of individual workers, even though that's the normal assumption. This relationship may be understood by clarifying those separate goals.

Company Goals

Ordinarily, goals of a company, or other business entities, are clear and often officially stated in the charter or the mission statement. Although there may be many goals stated by a company, such as: to improve the quality of life, to enhance the environment, to create a good working environment, to provide a higher level of service or to be the leader in the field; the real goal of a company is profit. And, profit is not a bad or a negative goal for a company, for if a company is not profitable it can't survive to create more career opportunities for individual workers.

The creation of conflict is enhanced when companies lack the courage to proclaim that profit is the major goal. Many companies feel their goals must sound enchanting, altruistic, and socially supportive in an attempt to camouflage the real motive of profit. This absence of clarity raises false hopes by workers and society that the purpose for the organization is for their personal enhancement, for that's what many proclaimed company goals suggest.

An honest and fair goal announced by a company might eliminate much of the conflict that's perpetuated in that company. Perhaps a simple and honest goal wouldn't give false hopes to many vulnerable workers encouraged to believe the company exists only for their career development, if they remain loyal and dedicated workers.

A simple, honest, and socially fair goal might be: To make a profit, within socially regulated or socially accepted standards. A goal this simple wouldn't suggest or imply to workers by false innuendo that the company would individually and specifically care for their personal needs. Workers, as well as other members of society, must learn for themselves that company profits are necessary for society to grow to develop more career opportunities for all members of society. The word *profit* must be displayed in a glass case rather than stored secretly in a dark dungeon.

Now, the question of executive greed is a consideration if the concept of profit as *good* is accepted. This concept must be considered in two dimensions; first, as a social contribution and secondly, as a personal contribution.

As a social contribution profit must exist for a company to create opportunities in the form of job expansion. If jobs aren't increased in both quantity and quality, then opportunities for more people who need those jobs aren't available for more individual careers. Profit is the base of opportunities.

As a personal contribution it really doesn't matter technically or economically if greed by some executives drives that profit motive, as long as profit develops to increase more opportunities for more people. This idea might seem somewhat strange, but consider the use of excess and disposable money.

Income earned through salary and bonuses in excess of that required for basic subsistence is considered discretionary income. A small amount of discretionary income is ordinarily used by the average person to buy special amenities such as a larger automobile, a boat, a travel trailer, or a larger house. When those normal desires have been filled, the excess discretionary income must be put somewhere; it cannot be put into one's wallet, and it's not ordinarily buried in a tin can in the back yard.

This excess discretionary income is ordinarily invested back into the economy to create more job opportunities or to create loans to create more job opportunities. Under simple economic theory, as jobs are increased the demand for workers also increases, which results in better working conditions and higher wages to attract those more qualified workers.

Although it might seem unfair that many executives are paid more than they are obviously worth it really doesn't matter, for they are forced to return that excess money back into the economy. They can't eat it and it's doubtful they burn it for warmth. Their normal use for it is usually only to worry about losing it. Although the excess money belongs to them, it doesn't belong to them, for other people use it for better purposes.

The purpose for this discussion of corporate goals is not to suggest that it's reasonable and fair for corporate leaders to be paid excessive salaries and bonuses. The purposes for this discussion is to emphasize that real corporate goals should be honestly stated, and there's nothing wrong with profit being one of those goals; and, to suggest that workers shouldn't de-motivate themselves by comparing their income with that of corporate executives. All those things that high-paid corporate executives buy and own are really controlled by others to make more career opportunities available in society.

Mid-Management Goals

Goals at the mid-management level have a different character. These goals must directly support company goals, but often become frustrated because company policy doesn't always follow company goals. Company goals ordinarily are established by long-term thinking and grand design, but company policies to support those goals often are more focused on quarterly results. This condition is particularly intensified if autocratic leaders occupy the senior leadership positions.

This condition causes mid-management goals to be unclear or even non-existent. This is the basis of a condition often referred to as the mid-management crisis. Leaders at this level often feel they are responsible for conditions they cannot control, for that control has been taken from them by bureaucracy and shifting priorities.

Ordinarily, however, mid-level leaders have some flexibility to establish discretionary goals within their departments that give those leaders a feeling of personal success when they accomplish those personal discretionary goals. If the company accomplishes its goals, these mid-level leaders are rewarded with a feeling of achievement for being part of that success by the company. If the leader accomplishes his or her personal discretionary goals, that leader is rewarded with a feeling of personal success for that accomplishment.

Worker Goals

The most critical and the least understood goals in a work environment are workers' goals. The lack of understanding of workers' goals by leaders, and by workers themselves, is undoubtedly the impetus for the highest conflict in the work environment. This problem persists because workers' goals haven't been analyzed as a subject that should be separated from company goals. It's long been assumed that, "What's good for the company is good for the workers."

Although there's an interdependent relationship, it's not a totally supportive relationship. As suggested earlier, workers are hired into a job with the understanding they automatically assume the goals of the company. That assumption goes further and suggests that if workers assume those goals that they will automatically be rewarded with a successful career. Only part of this assumption is valid.

If workers assume company goals as their own, the maximum reward they should anticipate is a feeling of achievement for being part of an accomplishment. This feeling of achievement, although a good feeling for a while, has nothing in common with a worker's personal career or success.

Furthermore, workers ordinarily have no areas of personal discretion to assign themselves discretionary goals in the workplace that will give themselves a feeling of personal success. Things workers do ordinarily are parts of whole functions and, as such, don't permit workers to see their finished products even if they could assign personal and discretionary goals for themselves. Their goals, if they have the discretion to designate any, are more often controlled by a leader. Workers simply have no opportunities for personal success in the normal workplace, only an opportunity for a partial feeling of achievement.

The tragedy of this dilemma isn't that workers are incapable of assigning success goals for themselves, for many workers do; and those workers usually have great successes. The tragedy is that the general understanding of the workplace is that worker goals aren't necessary, for that workplace will provide enough opportunities if the worker will be a good worker.

This erroneous understanding isn't isolated only in the workplace, it's also reinforced by pressures from society. Society encourages workers to be 'good dedicated workers,' and suggests that if they are they will be rewarded with successful careers. Society even places legislative restrictions on business and industrial leaders to make this happen. For example, there are many restrictions that protect 'job rights.'

This hidden incompatibility of company goals versus worker goals, or the assumption that company goals should be worker goals is the incongruity that produces the popular condition of worker alienation. Worker alienation, when workers feel they are an insignificant part of a whole process and that they have no control over their lives, becomes the vague battlefield of workplace conflict.

This battlefield, this vagueness, can easily and simply be eliminated or, at the very minimum, reduced. Workers must understand, probably through training in the workplace, that they must have personal success goals for themselves. For without a plan for personal success they will have no other alternative than to feel alienated.

Although this alienation is most often attributed to the conditions and the actions of the workplace, the real sources of this alienation should be identified and acknowledged so they may be corrected. They are: (1) the assumption that the workplace is a supportive career place, and (2) the absence of personal worker goals to develop a career.

To develop meaningful goals, however, goals must be understood. The purpose for the next section is to make goals clear and meaningful, so self-assigned goals may be useful.

Meaningful Goals

Personal success is determined by accomplishing goals. If a person doesn't assign himself or herself goals then that person cannot accomplish those goals. Instead of having a plan for success, one will have a definite plan for failure.

A misunderstanding of goals, however, may also cause failure. People are often advised by parents, teachers, or other authority figures to assign goals to themselves, but many of them can't do that clearly enough to establish a target for success. Understanding goals is important in the process of assigning goals to oneself, for one might think he or she has assigned a goal when, in fact, that person hasn't assigned a goal.

Goals may be identified by two types and two dimensions. The two clearly identifiable types of goals include short-term goals and long-term goals. This concept of short-term and long-term goals seems simple enough, but people often fail to become successful because they don't understand the relationship between these two types of goals.

Short-term goals must be set to accomplish long-term goals. Often a person will assign himself or herself a long-term goal that's so distant it becomes unreachable. Long-term goals are reached only by assigning and reaching a series of short-term goals. Not only must long-term goals be reached by accomplishing short-term goals, the reinforcement of success by accomplishing each of those short-term goals makes the possibility of reaching the long-term goal a reality. The success process is learned through achieving short-term goals. The long-term goal evolves naturally.

Successfully achieving long-term goals is determined by achieving a series of short-term goals. If it's that simple why isn't it easy for everyone to become successful? It is easy for everyone to become successful, however, there's usually one major problem. That major problem is to take the first step to accomplish the first short-term goal. Unsuccessful people fail to take that first simple step. Let's consider a common example.

Many high school students plan to get a college degree, however, only a few follow through to reach that goal. The difference in whether a person gets a college degree is usually not determined by desire, by cost, by need, or by intelligence. That success is more often determined by the simple fact that some graduates assign a short-term goal of going to the college to enroll. Others only plan to go to the college to enroll - someday.

Another reason some high school graduates don't get their college degree is that they cannot wait to get the degree. Each individual course is considered an insurmountable obstacle rather than a short-term goal. Those who fail focus on the long-term dream and not the realistic short-term goals of each individual course.

Although understanding the differences and inferences of short-term goals and long-term goals is important, there are other equally important considerations of goals. These include the dimensions of definite and indefinite goals.

Often, one thinks he or she has assigned himself or herself a goal when, in fact, that hasn't occurred. That person might have assigned an indefinite goal which is really not an attainable goal. The two important dimensions of goals include the *definite* and the *indefinite.*

A definite goal is one that may be clearly described, identified and achieved or reached. It's also one that may be measured in steps of completion along the way.

For example, how many times have you heard someone say, "My goal in life is to save enough money to retire on when I get old so I can live happily ever after?" This common statement, belief or anticipation is a primary cause of failure for many people who would like to succeed. There's a fundamental flaw with this goal, however, that makes it unreachable. That fundamental flaw is that this isn't really a goal. It can't be measured, and it can't be understood if it's reached.

Two concepts make this goal unreachable. First, many people never feel they are old. At what age would a person consider as the right age for that goal? Secondly, the exact amount of money needed for retirement hasn't been stated. Is it $100,000, $200,000 or two million dollars? Clearly, this common idea isn't a goal, for it can't be measured along the way or identified when it's achieved.

A definite goal would be, "I plan to save $100,000 and retire when I reach the age of 65." Both conditions may be identified and may be measured between the beginning and the ending. At age 55, a person would know that he or she has only ten more years until that planned retirement age. If that person had saved $30,000, then he or she would know that the money target is about thirty percent complete. This is a definite goal.

Workers don't fail to reach goals because they cannot reach those goals. They fail to reach goals because they only dream of long-term goals, they fail to assign clear short-term goals and they don't assign themselves definite and identifiable goals. Workers who fail don't understand the importance of adequately assigning and properly striving to reach simple goals. They tend to over-dramatize and over-complicate a simple process. Or, in many cases they've been allowed to believe that their workplaces will assign goals for them that will enhance their personal success.

Reconciling Goals

Before workplace conflict may be eliminated, goals - the basis for success - must be reconciled. In this process, it's important to acknowledge workplace goals will not create success for individual workers. Workplace goals are designed to permit success for a business, corporation, department, or workplace. Those goals are impersonal. Those goals are established for the fundamental survival of that workplace.

Not only are they usually not compatible with workers' personal success goals, often they're directly opposed to workers' personal goals. For example, massive layoffs often occur for a company to reach its goals. This certainly strongly suggests that company goals aren't designed for individual worker's success, although those workers might have been enticed to work for that company with the understood innuendo that the company was a 'people' company. This statement's not meant to criticize companies that use this approach, for the survival of companies is as important as the success of individual workers. If companies don't survive, workers have less opportunities for personal success.

Workers, as well as companies, must accept the personal responsibility to become more individually successful. To do this, however, they must realize that their success is their responsibility; and it doesn't happen by accident or simply because they're nice people. To become successful, one must deliberately plan to be successful, by achieving many short-range goals that develop into long-range success goals.

The alternative to a deliberate plan to be successful is a plan to be a deliberate failure. Let's analyze two examples that demonstrate these concepts:

Bennie, The Befuddled

Bennie was from a lower middle-income family. Both his parents worked and they earned enough money to be reasonably comfortable, although they didn't earn enough to take long vacations to far-away places. They were allowed two weeks for vacation each year, but they couldn't afford to travel over two or three hundred miles from home. They were making house payments, without any of their payments being late; and each had his and her automobile. They were also able to buy Bennie an older automobile when he became a senior in high school. They felt that he needed transportation for school and for part-time jobs that he found, occasionally. He also helped his parents with shopping, since both his parents worked.

Bennie found a regular job two weeks before he graduated from high school. His father's friend had recommended Bennie to his manager at the local tire distribution center. The friend had worked there for fifteen years, and his manager trusted his judgement about new workers.

During his job interview the manager told Bennie, "Bennie, this is a good place to work. Our company has been here for over thirty years and we have some good people here. Our people are dedicated and we return that dedication with good pay and a good work environment. We support our people and give them every opportunity for advancement if they show they are good workers.

This is a place that you can be proud of, and a place that you can develop a good career." The manager added, "Of course, you understand that if you aren't a good worker who can be at work on time, or if you cannot join our productive team, you won't be allowed to develop your career in our company."

Bennie thought this environment was the perfect place and the perfect job. The manager had told him essentially that, "If you do a good job for the company the company will provide you with a rewarding career." At that time the thought of a good career was important, but Bennie was more concerned with receiving his first pay envelope. He accepted the job without hesitation.

Two years later Bennie was doing the same job. He hadn't been promoted and he hadn't been moved to other jobs to broaden his knowledge and his career base. He was still moving tires from storage racks onto vans and trucks for shipment to delivery destinations. His job wasn't challenging, and certainly not exciting. Furthermore, he saw his manager only occasionally when the manager escorted visitors and clients through his area. Sometimes the manager didn't even acknowledge Bennie's existence or even say, "Hello, Bennie."

Bennie had received two pay increases since he began working for that company; however, those raises were just enough to cover normal inflation. He hadn't received any increase in buying power. He had also learned that promotions and advancements in the company were rare, since the workforce was stable and no new functions were ever created to offer more positions. The last supervisory position that had been filled was filled by an experienced supervisor from another company.

Bennie was becoming frustrated, for he didn't understand how he could advance and improve himself in the company if there were no opportunities in that company. His manager had told him that if he did a good job those opportunities would be there. Where were they?

In his frustration Bennie wanted to quit his job, but he couldn't. He learned that he needed more experience in his current field or more education to get another job that was at least equal in pay. His manager wouldn't let him do other functions to gain broader experiences, and he felt that he couldn't quit his job to get more education. He was married and had a child, so he now had a family to support.

What finally happened to Bennie? He continued to work at the same job. However, his attendance level dropped to the company average, he often missed work because he was 'sick,' and his productivity level decreased to the typical sixty percent for that workplace.

Bennie eventually increased his self-esteem in the organization though. He helped organize a union in his workplace and now he's the union representative for his department.

Carol, The Charger

Carol was a posting clerk who worked for a mid-size accounting firm. She had completed one year of college before she began a permanent job, but she had to quit college because her parents couldn't afford to send her past the first year. She had been working for the accounting firm for about six months when a new supervisor was hired for her department.

Her new supervisor, Melissa, had been a supervisor for another accounting firm for about three years, so she was already familiar with the standard supervisory role. Although she was a relatively hard taskmaster to insure that her department was productive, she was also concerned with the welfare of workers in her department. She had learned that progressive workers have less time or incentive to be problem workers.

Consequently, one of Melissa's first major tasks was to insure that each worker in her department was taught how to become a progressive and career-oriented worker. She held regular counseling and coaching sessions with each worker in her department to accomplish that purpose.

Carol was the third worker to attend the coaching session with Melissa. The first two workers who had talked with Melissa told Carol, "Oh, she just wants to talk about some goals or something like that - nothing important." Carol was anticipating the usual "how's it going" routine. She was surprised at what Melissa said during the interview.

Melissa told Carol, "Carol, since I've been here I've observed that you seem to be well-trained, efficient and dedicated to your job. Do you like your job as much as you seem to?"

Carol replied that she did, and added, "I was planning to get a college degree but things didn't work out, so I decided to get a job to start a working career." Carol added, "I really like this job and I'll probably make my career here if things keep going as well as they have for me." Carol was expecting Melissa to agree with her and to encourage her to plan on a long and rewarding career with that company, since the company was a good place to work and she seemed happy there. Instead, Carol was puzzled by Melissa's response.

Melissa said, "Carol, I appreciate your concern for the job, and I appreciate the fact that you know you can make a positive contribution to our company. Our company, any company, needs good and dedicated people like you. However, if you're concerned only about making a career and a contribution at this company, you might one day resent the fact that you gave more to this company than you gave to yourself. You must understand that the purpose for a company is to make a profit to survive. That doesn't always work to the best interests of its employees, including me." Melissa added, "Carol, you must also plan for your personal future - and you can do that while making a greater contribution to our company."

Carol asked, "What do you mean? I thought that if I remain a good worker, the best worker that I can be, and I stay out of trouble, that the company will recognize those contributions. Maybe some higher positions will come open that I can be promoted into one day."

Melissa answered, "How long do you think it will take for that possibility to happen? Are you really prepared to just wait as long as it takes, and only hope it happens? What will your attitude and your performance become if that possibility never happens?" She also added, "Do you really want to do this same job, forever? Will you remain happy and motivated in this same position when you're ten years older?"

Carol hesitated before she answered these questions, for she had never really given much thought to success and career alternatives. She had assumed that one simply goes to work for a company and tries to do a good job to become successful at that company. She was slowly beginning to understand what Melissa was suggesting. Finally, she answered, "Are you saying that I might advance my career somewhere else rather than here at this company? How can I do that?"

Melissa explained, "The company has goals that it must meet to survive. Some of those company goals will give you opportunities for personal success and personal advancement, and some of those goals might be detrimental to your personal career plans. There's no way to forecast, accurately, what might happen in the next year, five years or twenty years. If you want to be in control of your career and your success, you must take positive personal actions to advance yourself."

She explained further that Carol occupied the same position as the company regarding goals. "Carol, you should put yourself in a similar position that the company occupies. You should have goals that support your career, your success and your survival. In some cases those goals might support the survival of this company, and in some cases your goals might not support the survival of this company; but in either case you should have the same opportunity for success that this company has. You should not subordinate your goals for the survival of the company, for the company certainly wouldn't subordinate its goals for your survival."

Carol agreed with Melissa, "I'm sure you're right about that." She also asked, "What do you suggest?"

"What do you really want to do with your life? What would you consider success for yourself?"

Carol replied that she really didn't know what she wanted to do. She would have to "think about it for awhile."

Melissa encouraged her to think about some career plans until they had their next meeting. She told Carol she would help analyze those plans then or anytime Carol wanted to talk to her about her career.

These two examples of Bennie and Carol demonstrate two influences and considerations of goals in the workplace. Bennie's manager gave Bennie the usual and traditional hiring interview, which suggested that if Bennie remains a good worker he will automatically be rewarded with a good career. Since Bennie developed no 'self' goals, he eventually became de-motivated and evolved into a common source of low productivity and conflict.

Carol was fortunate to have a supervisor who understood the nature of goals, and who cared enough to try to help her workers become successful. Carol understood what Melissa said, and took her advice. Carol eventually completed her college degree through night school and correspondence courses. She was hired as a manager at another larger accounting firm in the same city.

Summary

Goals are important to success for organizations as well as for individuals. Success is impossible without goals for without goals there can be no goal achievement. A person or a company might accidentally accumulate wealth or things, but certainly the accumulation of things cannot be defined as success. Success is more encompassing than just things. Success must include a feeling of achievement and self-esteem from accomplishing goals.

Much workplace conflict that produces low productivity results from the absence of meaningful and clear goals, especially from the absence of workers' goals. Workers who have clear and progressive goals, and who are in sincere pursuit of those goals, have no time nor inclination to worry about the bad things that happen to them. They are too busy succeeding.

Other workers who wait for success to come to them, automatically through the workplace career process, have more time and inclination to find those things in the workplace that prevent their success. They wait for things to happen instead of making things happen. Waiting is their degenerative process. In this process, the negative things become more active and more visible. While those with goals advance those without goals fall behind, for they are doing nothing but 'being a good worker.'

Workplace conflict is almost always blamed on bad leaders by workers, and bad workers by leaders. These accusations are based on the principle that the other party must be at fault since, "I'm doing my best." That workplace conflict isn't caused by the basic 'badness' of either workers or leaders. That workplace conflict that destroys productivity in the workplace and aspirations for individuals is caused by the lack of a clear understanding of the importance and the power of clear and meaningful goals.

9

THE SUCCESS CIRCLE

Productivity and those harmonious relationships in a work environment that facilitate that productivity depend upon many factors. Perceptions and communications are the basics that form the foundation for relationships that result in harmony and productivity.

Those perceptions are formed from many sources and influences. Some of these influences have been described in the previous chapters. Perceptions of leaders are varied and different, as are perceptions of workers. Each person, leader or worker, carries a complete and unique encyclopedia of perceptions, knowledge, opinions, values, and ideas in his or her mind.

Sometimes these individual and personal books may be opened and read. More often, however, those personal books remain closed, secretive, and defensive. To develop the cooperation and consensus of those goals needed in a workplace to reach optimum productivity, leaders and workers must learn how to read the other's personal encyclopedia. It's not necessary to read the complete encyclopedia, only those parts that apply to goals, productivity, and personal achievement.

Two fundamental prerequisites are necessary, however, to understand the other person's encyclopedia, those beliefs and perceptions formed within one's mind, even when it may be exposed and read. First, the owner of that encyclopedia must have clear beliefs and perceptions. Secondly, the reader of that encyclopedia must be open, sincere, and knowledgeable in the reading process. The owner of that encyclopedia may be a leader, a worker, or any other person who might contribute to harmony or conflict in an organization. Let's analyze these concepts further.

The Encyclopedia Owner

The encyclopedia owner, the person to be understood, must have clear beliefs and perceptions if that person may be understood. Of course, this doesn't mean that a psychoanalysis must occur to understand the basic and most intimate workings of that individual. This concept means that for another person to function within a range of acceptability of that person, the other person must know what the owner of the encyclopedia routinely expects and anticipates.

If that person has no clear philosophy of life, leadership, cooperation, or human relations; that person cannot have a consistent pattern that allows another person to understand and anticipate.

Without a clear anticipation or expectation of one, the other cannot adjust to accommodate those anticipations into his or her beliefs, ideas, and concepts. A meeting of the minds - a merging of those books - cannot occur to offer common areas of understanding that permit effective communications, negotiation, and cooperation. Without a meeting of the minds a larger conflict zone in any organization, or in any human relationship, is inevitable. One of the basis of this clear synthesis must be a consistent encyclopedia that's based on clearly established beliefs. A confused or vague book cannot be read with meaning. If one doesn't understand himself or herself neither can anyone else.

The Encyclopedia Reader

The encyclopedia reader is another important part of workplace understanding, and either harmony or conflict in that workplace. The encyclopedia reader tries to understand how to adjust his or her actions to fit into the framework of the beliefs and expectations of the other person. The reader may also be either a leader, a worker, or any other person who has any interest in the productivity of an organization and the relationships within an organization.

Assuming the encyclopedia owner has a clear book that may easily be read, the reader may still not interpret that reading properly. This ordinarily occurs when the reader attempts to interpret that book by using his or her own set of values, beliefs, and ideas; without considering the other person might have different values, beliefs, and ideas.

If the reader who fails to consider the other person's book is a leader, this reader ordinarily tends to develop more autocratic and belligerent actions. This person assumes workers are stupid and lazy and have no comprehension of rational responsibilities. This person creates a wider conflict zone.

If the reader who fails to consider the other person's book is a worker, or a subordinate, this person often becomes desperate, defeated, frustrated, and often alienated. Either of these reactions reduces the level of effective communications in an organization and ultimately increases the conflict zone in that organization.

In summary, people's perceptions and beliefs in an organization are vital to the cooperative relationships that allow harmony to develop, or to be maintained, within an organization. Ordinarily, the person under scrutiny or evaluation is the person blamed or charged with lack of understanding or lack of cooperation. In fact, the person who does the evaluating or who forms the opinion of the other person might be more at fault for that lack of cooperation and understanding; for that person might be forming opinions through a faulty perspective.

Leaders and workers are vulnerable to this faulty perspective. No one is immune, and no one fails to contribute his or her share to the conflict in many workplaces.

In fairness, however, some common influences and pressures should be recognized that cause many leaders and workers to act in a manner that doesn't reflect their true characters. Leaders are often forced by higher authorities, or by unusual productivity demands, to change leadership character. Workers are often forced by peer pressure to do certain things or to act in certain ways that don't reflect their real perspectives or beliefs. Under these unusual conditions each personal encyclopedia might be clear, but their book covers remain closed.

Each encyclopedia of perspectives, beliefs and expectations in an organization must be clear, open, and read with sincere objectivity before effective and productive communications may develop. These clear and effective communications are necessary to eliminate the zone of conflict that exists in most organizations. This enhanced communications process will be analyzed next.

Productive Communications

Things happen in an organization, as well as in most other places, through an interaction of communications. Communications are necessary to convey plans, to explain procedures, to provide coordination and support, to create visualization of the purpose or the end product of those activities, and to show a reasonable justification for those things to be done. These reasonable causes are often called motivations.

Communications in an organization are also necessary to express feelings and emotions among people in those organizations. These emotional and special communications are required to create unity of purpose in the organization and to eliminate those burdensome problems in the work environment that aren't job-related. These burdensome problems are most frequently related to individual personalities and opposing interests at any given point in time.

For example, at any given point in time when a worker is most needed on the job, that worker might have personal interests that demand he or she be elsewhere. Another opposing interest would be the absence of a success plan or the frustration of trying to accomplish that success plan by a worker. These conditions add to the natural tendency for a workplace to remain in conflict.

To accomplish these purposes of the communications process, communications must be considered from two aspects, or from two dimensions. The first dimension would consider a person's basic ability to communicate clearly. The second dimension would consider the person's ability to communicate productively.

Communicating Clearly

One's ability to communicate clearly and effectively is acknowledged as one of the major factors that contribute to a person's success, the success of an organization, and employee comfort in the work environment. Without good communications a productive work environment and harmonious relationships aren't likely to exist. Clarity in the communications process is a fundamental requirement for those effective communications.

Historically, the burden of effective communications in the workplace has been a direct leadership responsibility. The same logic suggesting leaders must be in control to manipulate and force workers to be motivated and successful applies to the question of good communications. Historically, that's also been assumed and accepted as the total responsibility of leaders.

Workers and other subordinates are equally as responsible for good communications in an organization as are supervisors and managers. Communication is as basic to employeeship as it is to leadership. Things happen in workplaces that must be communicated up the line to management, as well as things that must be communicated down the line to workers.

This communication process must be shared equally if the workplace is to be harmonious and successful. As a worker, one cannot assume the attitude, "I just work here." Each member of the organization, including workers, must demonstrate the approach, "I work here and I'm doing my part to make this the best place to work."

Workers, as well as leaders, must learn to communicate effectively if they expect their ideas and suggestions to be considered by their leaders. Many workers know of problems before they become obvious to management; or, they know answers to resolve existing problems. If they don't know how to express their ideas to people who can implement those ideas, two negative conditions occur. First, workers will become frustrated, for those good ideas cannot be understood to be used. Secondly, the ideas or suggestions might be good ones to solve real problems, but they might never be revealed.

The following list of basic elements of communication may help those weak in communication skills to become more effective and persuasive in getting their ideas accepted by others. These are ideas presented in most communications training classes:

The purpose must be clear. One must have an understood purpose for communications. The purpose should be to inform, to amuse, to inquire, to resolve a problem, or to request assistance. If one's purpose isn't clear to himself or herself, it usually will not be clear to anyone else. One should ask himself or herself, "Do I want to talk to that person to inform, or do I want to ask a question."

For example, suppose a grocery clerk is stocking shelves in a grocery store. The clerk opens a carton that's marked 'beans.' As the clerk removes these cans of beans from the carton to put them onto the shelf, the clerk notices that the labels on the cans are marked 'corn.' Just then the supervisor happens to walk by, and the clerk knows he should tell the supervisor about the packaging error. There are many ways the clerk can tell the supervisor that there has been a packaging error. Here are some options:

"Hey, Boss, are they putting corn in bean boxes, now?"

"Hey, Boss, those packaging people did it again."

"Hey, Boss, we got corn mixed with beans."

"Hey, Boss, I just opened a carton of beans, and the can labels said it was corn."

Since the purpose for this information is to tell the supervisor there's a problem in labeling of beans or corn, the last statement, above, most clearly fulfills that purpose. The other statements are unclear and vague for that purpose.

Without a definite purpose, there can be no effective communications. The communication should convey its own purpose, either by clear implication or by direct statement.

There must be a listener. For effective communications, one must have an active listener, or a receiver, of what one is saying. If someone is talking and the listener's not really listening, then the person talking isn't communicating. If a person has something important to say, and that person wants it understood, he or she must insure the listener is prepared to listen. How is this done? Four simple questions may be asked to determine if the listener is ready to listen.

The first question: Is the listener familiar with the subject to be discussed? If the listener is familiar with the subject, the familiarity will help make that listener ready to listen. If he or she isn't familiar with the subject, getting the listener ready to listen may require more effort.

The second question: Does the listener have time to listen at that time? If the listener doesn't have time to listen then, one will be wasting effort with those words. If the speaker's not sure that the listener has time, the speaker should simply ask. The discussion might have more effect at a later time.

The third question: Does the listener have any interest in what the speaker is saying? If not, the speaker might have to explain why this subject concerns the listener before going into specific details of the subject.

The fourth question: Does the speaker have the full attention of the listener? The listener can interpret the full intention of the discussion only if he or she is attentive to what the speaker is saying. If the listener is doing other work while the speaker is talking, effective communications will not be achieved. In this case the speaker should volunteer to wait until the listener is ready to listen.

The fact that a person is talking doesn't mean that effective communications are taking place. One's listener must be actively trying to receive, correctly, what the speaker is trying to say, correctly. The speaker must get the listener prepared to do that.

The situation must be appropriate. The situation is also important for someone to communicate effectively. One must consider where he or she is and what that person and the listener are doing at that time. One must also consider the complexity of the subject being discussed.

For example, one shouldn't discuss something that's private in a place or situation where other people might overhear the conversation. The private subject could pertain to the speaker, the listener, another person or another event. The listener, or others, might become uncomfortable. Effective communications in this situation would certainly be difficult.

A real Don Juan might find it difficult to communicate effectively if he is talking about dinner, moonlight, and romance in an area where heavy machinery is noisily at work. The situation just wouldn't be right. At this time, a Don Juan wants to be at his best. Distractions would certainly create communications problems.

Effective communications are enhanced if one insures those communications take place in the right situation - the right subject, at the right time, at the right place.

Perceptions must be considered. One's unique storehouse of knowledge and information can affect the way that person receives and interprets what someone says. That person may listen, intently, to what one is saying. That listener might be giving his or her total interest and concentration, and the conversation might be taking place in the right situation. The speaker might be speaking clearly and completely. Even with all this, one might not be communicating effectively, if the listener's background and perceptions are different from those of the speaker.

Perhaps that person is from a background that included a defensive environment. In this case, discussions meant for that person's information might be received as an argument. The listener's perceptions require that listener to defend his or her position. An argument or defensive position wasn't the purpose or intent for that information.

Other perception problems result from opinion words such as: big, small, immediately, as soon as possible and when you get a chance. These words can mean different things, depending upon one's perception. A person's background often determines that persons definition of different words.

Information should be organized. Information should be organized if it's to be presented in a way that will produce desired results. Most communications, whether written or spoken, should have at least three parts: an introduction, a discussion and a conclusion.

The information should be presented in that order, with the introduction first, the discussion next, and the conclusion last. If a person has the discussion part first, without an introduction, the listener or reader may find it difficult to determine what the speaker is talking about. If the introduction is at the end, the listener might think that one plans to say more, and will be puzzled if the statement is not completed.

For the introduction, one may simply state what he or she is talking about. For example, "Joe, I would like to talk with you about giving me some help today." In the discussion, one should give reasons, such as, "You don't seem to be too busy in your department, and I'm two days behind in my department." For the conclusion, one should present a clear question, "Think you can give me some help?"

This is a simple example, of course, of an organized communication. Nevertheless, it serves the purpose of explaining the method and importance of organizing to make the most effective presentation.

Proper emphasis is essential. To become a successful communicator, one must also learn to use appropriate emphasis. There are two kinds of emphasis that must be considered. First is the emphasis on the degree of urgency. This means how soon, or how strongly an action should be taken. For example, if a woman sees a mouse in her house, she wants to get rid of it 'right now.' The degree of force should also be considered. This means a cannon isn't required to get rid of that mouse. Probably a shoe, if quick enough, is sufficient force to eliminate a mouse. One should save most of the excitement for topics that need it, and save the big guns for the elephants.

The second type of emphasis concerns differentiation of time, space, material, procedures, and other similar matters. A speaker wouldn't emphasize time, if money is really the topic. One wouldn't emphasize procedures if the real topic is people.

To improve communications skills one should keep emphasis in proper order, priority, and degree. Emphasis may then be used as an effective tool. If that tool is used improperly, it loses its value.

Communication requires clarity. Some speakers may talk to someone for ten minutes without the receiver really understanding what that person is talking about. This situation is a common occurrence. It's a problem of not communicating with clarity.

There are three basic causes for lacking clarity in communications. They are: not using proper sentence structure, talking in endless circles, and mumbling. The importance of organizing thoughts into three parts: the introduction, the discussion and the conclusion was discussed previously.

Organizing sentences properly is just as important. A speaker must have three parts to a sentence, for that sentence to be clear. A sentence must have a subject, a verb, and a predicate; or a clear implication of the missing part. A subject, verb or predicate tells who did what, what happened to something or what happened to someone. All three parts are essential to provide clarity.

Talking in circles also prevents successful communications. Some speakers repeat statements without an ending to insure the listener becomes overwhelmed with the facts. Their endless chant is regenerated with key words such as, "You know," "and, uh," "like this," "like I said," and "believe me." These conversations not only lose their clarity, they quickly become boring.

People who mumble, by definition, lack clarity. One should suspect he or she might be a mumbler if other people frequently ask, "What did you say?" "Sorry, I didn't understand." If one gets this reaction frequently, he or she should analyze his or her speech effectiveness. In this case, a tape recorder would be useful.

Proper grammar is necessary. Correct grammar is a basic essential of effective communications. A person is not required to be an English teacher to know enough of the English basics to be effective. However, one should know enough basic grammar to speak or write, in most situations, in a manner that's not conspicuous.

Using proper grammar is essential for two reasons. First, without it a person will not have enough self-confidence to be comfortable in many situations that require discussion. That person will deprive himself or herself of possible career advancement opportunities. One also deprives his or her company from positive information or ideas that the person might have.

Secondly, use of improper grammar is an indication of a poor or weak education level. One's ideas and comments will have little credibility if that person's apparent education level doesn't support the background of those ideas. One's ideas might not be taken seriously if that person sounds as if he or she doesn't know what he or she is talking about.

If one plans a successful career, bad grammar will be a handicap. To succeed, one must have the capability to communicate. While in this communication process, a person must demonstrate confidence, knowledge, and ability. Bad grammar, since it cannot be hidden, will work against one's efforts to be successful.

Correct grammar is easy to learn, with minimum effort. If one feels weak in this area, he or she can get adequate help from a basic English course, or even from self study guides.

Listener feedback is required. Reactions from the listener is a good source to determine if one is communicating effectively. The speaker should watch the listener's reactions and mannerisms. Is the listener looking at the speaker, or is that listener playing with the telephone? Is the listener nodding agreement and disagreement, or does he or she seem disinterested? Is the listener asking questions or offering ideas? These are clues and indicators that will help a speaker determine if communications are effective.

A person must communicate effectively if that person plans or wants to be successful, and to be a successful part of a harmonious work group without conflict. Clear and effective communications help reduce that conflict for clear words and thoughts express clear intentions and ideas, not intentions and ideas that may be interpreted as negative by another person who ordinarily expects most things to be negative. Clear and effective communications leave less opportunity for misinterpretation.

Once this first dimension of clear communications has been achieved, however, a person must concentrate on the second dimension of communications to enhance the communications process. Productive communications will be analyzed next.

Communicating Productively

Although the ability to communicate clearly is required of every person in the work environment who hopes to become successful, that ability alone isn't enough to assure success. Members of the work environment must also use that ability for a purpose, and that purpose is mutual productivity. That productivity must be toward the goals of the company and the goals of each member of the work environment.

Productive communications may occur only when communications are used openly, sincerely, courteously and without hesitation or ulterior motives. Each worker and each leader in the organization must assume that what he or she says in that work environment is accepted by other members for the purpose of harmonious productivity. The suspicion of ulterior and selfish motives must be eliminated from the work environment for that environment to assume productive communications.

A working model is needed to demonstrate this condition of harmonious and productive communications; which is the only conditions that will allow full productivity. This communications and productivity model will be identified as the *Success Circle*.

The Success Circle

The working model that explains the concept of communications that produce maximum productivity is based on four words. These four words outline the full scope of relationships in the work environment; and when organized in a comprehensive manner, give meaning to the idea of maximum productivity through harmonious cooperation.

Two generations of management theorists have understood the meanings of these words. They have also talked and written volumes about these words in vague and disconnected generalities. Most of the effort by these theorists, however, has been in specific areas of

175

educational or intellectual expertise by each of those recognized specialists. These words have not been joined in harmony through a combination of study, research, and practical application. This model demonstrates how these applications are combined to create a synthesis.

The following explanation of the circle of success theory wouldn't be possible without the background information and studies of many educators and motivation experts, too numerous to identify individually. Many, however, may be identified in the bibliography. This circle of success explanation is based on a synthesis of that background information, and experience involving organizational interrelationships.

Four Key Relationship Words

These four words that determine the effectiveness of an organization include: *confidence, risk, action* and *results.* Productivity, quality, and harmony in a work environment are ultimately determined by the level of understanding and the sincerity of application of these words. Those leaders who easily identify with the concepts of human relations management will easily absorb and synthesize the ideas of the circle of success into their logic. The more autocratic, or authoritarian, leaders might be somewhat more skeptical. Leadership styles and their implications are discussed in another chapter.

An experienced leader might observe these four words have no bearing or relationship to the idea or concept of good morale. Words that would refer to morale intentionally were ignored by this model. There's an important reason for this deletion. Historical studies and empirical research fail to prove a direct relationship between good morale and high productivity. The word morale must not be used interchangeably with pride, for there's a clear relationship between pride and productivity. The results of this model are intended to be increased success, pride, productivity, and harmony. High morale may or may not result.

Confidence. Confidence is the first word on the success circle. Confidence must, by definition, be the first word; for risk, action, and results will not occur unless confidence permits those things to happen. There are four relationships of confidence between only two people in a work environment. These four relationships will be identified individually and pertain only to confidence relationship factors between a worker and a leader. It should be acknowledged, however, that these relationships also exist between workers and between leaders.

First, is the confidence a worker feels toward himself or herself. It includes those questions from one's self of social class, intelligence, educational level, experience, and preparation.

Second, is the confidence a leader has within himself or herself. A leader's self-analysis factors include the same factors as a worker's. A leader's confidence is also affected by company support, economic restraints, and personal image.

Third, is the confidence the worker feels toward the leader. The worker must consider if his or her efforts will be properly recognized and fairly and justly rewarded. The worker also considers if the leader is supportive, truthful, honest, and reliable in times of added pressure or crisis.

Fourth, is the confidence the leader feels toward the worker. The leader must consider the worker's self-motivation, honesty, loyalty, dedication, and ability to perform required tasks.

It's interesting to observe that although there are four considerations of confidence in the relationship between a leader and a worker, only one of these relationships is routinely evaluated in work environments. This evaluation is closely related to the confidence the leader considers toward a worker. This evaluation is vaguely assigned by superiors on subordinates' performance reports. The word 'confidence' isn't specifically listed on those evaluation forms, however, the overall judgmental evaluation implies the level of the evaluator's confidence. Those performance reports will be analyzed later.

Risk. The ability and the desire to take risks are nurtured by high confidence. Although the word risk seems simple, it also has implications that must be shared between leaders and subordinates.

Leader. For a leader to accept a risk of doing something that's unusual (different, progressive, forceful) that leader must be supported by two high confidence factors. One is the confidence the leader has in himself or herself. The other is the confidence the leader has toward the subordinate.

Worker. A subordinate also considers two confidence factors before taking risks (full productivity, dedication, loyalty, support.) These include the subordinate's personal self-confidence, and the confidence the subordinate has toward the leader.

These risk factors must be resolved before progressive plans may be formed to expect full participative efforts. Leaders must have the risk of apathy and reluctance by those workers eliminated. Subordinates must have the feeling of unfairness and exploitation eliminated. These are the basis of those risk factors.

Action. Those confidence levels of, and between, leaders and workers must be high and positive to allow each to take the risk of maximum action. Leaders must plan action without the consideration that workers will not give their full efforts. Workers must give their best efforts without the fear and apprehension they will be unfairly treated or exploited.

Leaders and workers must take positive goal-oriented action. For either to be reluctant or hesitant, full commitment and full efficiency cannot occur. Furthermore, any reluctance to assume full action toward productivity is an indication that conflict exists in the organization.

Results. Confidence, risk, and action properly understood and pro-actively used will produce results. Achievement of results will continue the circle of success.

- Results will create more confidence.
- Confidence will permit more risks.
- More acceptance of risk will result in more efficient action.
- More efficient action will produce more results.

This circle of success concept isn't as complex or as theoretical as it might first appear. When the right combination of confidence factors develop and mature, those other words; risk, action, and results occur automatically.

Many progressive work environments have this circle of success, without it being specifically identified and labeled as such. Other work environments that seek improvement and increased productivity must focus on specific application of each word. The success circle may be started at any place on that circle - on either word.

Those four words: confidence, risk, action, and results also affect the viability and value of performance appraisal reports. This relationship will be analyzed in the next chapter.

Summary

Success for an organization, as well as success for each individual in that organization, is dependent upon mutual and cooperative relationships within that organization. Those mutual and cooperative relationships must not be based solely upon the abilities and the 'goodness' of those people in that organization. They must also be based upon the quality of communications that occur within that organization to express those abilities and that goodness.

This quality of communications exists only when two conditions occur. One of those conditions is that everyone must be involved in the communications process; and, those who are involved in the communications process must be able to express what they mean. They shouldn't allow their inadequacies of communication to cause misinterpretation of their thoughts. Each communicator must have the ability to insure the listener can interpret exactly what the speaker meant.

The second condition of quality communications demands communications and relationships within an organization be initiated and conveyed with sincerity and honesty of purpose. That purpose must be for the benefit of the organization and for individuals in the organization. Communications shouldn't be used for revenge, subterfuge, or any other selfish motives that would inhibit the ability of the organization to reach its highest level of potential success. That communications quality should also permit individuals within the organization to reach their highest potential. Of course, each individual would be responsible for determining his or her personal level of achievement.

Finally, a circle of success may be developed in any organization through effective and productive communications. Only after that communications quality is developed may the key words of success be formed into a clear success model. Those key words that form the success model, the circle, include: confidence, risk, action and results.

10

THE JUDGMENT CALL

Performance Appraisal Reports

The last chapter analyzed the importance of effective communications toward achieving positive results in the work environment. That chapter concluded that optimum productivity cannot be achieved without naturally honest and goal-oriented communications. There's an intrinsic flaw in the communications flow within many organizations that blocks the development of honest and mutual communications. That flaw, that block, is the performance appraisal process.

Many organizations are aware that effective communications are important in determining productivity and success. Many of those organizations have training programs, crusades, seminars, and even parties and athletic events to encourage more open and effective communications between and among workers and leaders. Most of these ideas and attempts to force good communications into an organization are usually futile.

There are ordinarily two major causes of conflict resulting from ineffective communications. The cause that occupies the top of that negative list is leadership actions contradictory to leadership promises, or implied promises. The second cause of things that restrict effective communications within an organization is the performance appraisal process.

These aren't the two most negative characteristics of an organization that create conflict; these are the two that are associated with the communications process. The top contributors of conflict in an organization remain leadership mediocrity, acceptance of that mediocrity by higher leaders, lack of effective employeeship and absence of respect for workers by leaders.

The appraisal process ordinarily isn't considered a focus, or a centralization, of the communications process in a workplace. Many leaders consider the appraisal process as an administrative chore that must be performed once or twice a year. Some leaders who perform the rating process do so only as a passing thought among the 'more important work' that's piled in their 'in' basket.

The rating process might be the most important part of the real productivity process. During this process, the leader is forced to see each worker face-to-face, and acknowledge each worker's existence. For some leaders, this is the only time they actually take to talk with their workers, individually.

This is also an important event in many workers' lives. Some workers don't have the confidence to initiate conversations with the boss, consequently, this is the only opportunity those workers have to let the boss know who they are. Those who know they 'have done a good job' expect the boss to recognize that, and to show that recognition during the appraisal interview process.

Two perspectives ordinarily exist during the typical appraisal interview. The rater hopes the ratee will quickly sign the rating form to acknowledge he or she has seen the form, and has been interviewed by the rater. The rater also hopes the ratee doesn't have any difficult questions that might cause conflict. The ratee hopes the rater has seen enough of his or her performance to give the high rating he or she deserves. When the rating is lower than the ratee expects, that worker assumes the leader doesn't really know his or her real value, or that the leader is callous and unfair.

The ratee who gets the highest rating, naturally, is always pleased. It's not unusual, however, for these workers to be well known by the leader who assigns the rating. It's also not unusual for less known workers, those who have more subdued personalities, to be assigned lower ratings, regardless of their level of effort and productivity.

In defense of the rater, there are situations where a real level of effort and productivity cannot be objectively determined, for example on an assembly line where the line moves at a standard pace. If everyone on that line makes no mistakes are they all perfect, are they all average, or are they all lazy?

The appraisal interview process should be a catalyst to improved communications that results in more harmony and productivity. It's not. It's now a process that results in tragedy, conflict, and withheld productivity.

The common evaluation and appraisal process used in business and industry is a productivity tragedy, as well as a personal tragedy. This process is not only one-dimensionally judgmental and the source of latent conflict, it usually results in assignment of the highest level of performance one might reach for himself or herself.

Management and motivation experts, as well as personnel managers, have been so focused on improving and redefining form maintenance, form documentation, and form meaning that the need to develop a positive and meaningful procedure has been obscured. A performance evaluation process shouldn't be so focused on the process, and the documentation and justification for that process, that it becomes counter-productive; which is the condition the normal evaluation process has achieved.

Performance appraisal reports are theoretically designed to acknowledge patterns and trends, to encourage good performance, and to prevent curiosity and conflict. The current process fails miserably, for it focuses on personalities, events, and defensive justifications, rather than focusing on improved methods and improved communications to encourage productivity. Disadvantages of traditional formal performance appraisal systems include:

They are subjective and judgmental.

They are often based on narrow perceptions.

They are oppressive in nature.

They review past performance - not next performance.

They invite negative behavior.

They assign the ratee's future performance level.

They destroy young aspirations.

Their effectiveness is often determined by the rater's ability.

This analysis of performance appraisals considers traditional appraisal forms as well as the more current exotic forms intended to obscure the idea that they're judgmental. Some are based on individual factors and some are based on relative characteristics among all workers in a department. They will not be identified individually, by type, for they all have the same level of judgmental hypocrisy. Some names are merely designed to camouflage this fact.

Purpose for Performance Appraisals

Individual performance appraisals are designed to assign a value for the performance and relative worth of a person to a company or some other business entity. Some organizations add to that purpose the desire to encourage an evaluated person to improve his or her performance. To achieve that expressed purpose, the typical rating form contains specific rating factors. These factors usually include:

Quantity of work produced

Quality of work produced

Knowledge of position

Planning and organizing ability

Awareness

Sense of urgency

Judgment

Cooperation

Dependability

Overall Rating

Each of these rating factors is typically assigned a rating number on a scale from one to ten. A rating below a six would indicate a weak performance in that area. A rating above an eight would indicate an exceptional performance. Some rating systems use other methods to assign comparative ratings by category of function, depending upon the number of employees rated.

For example, if a workplace has ten workers, each worker would be ranked one through ten in each of those evaluated functions. The overall rating for each individual would be the added score. Other equally strange, weird, and negative schemes have been devised to justify this judgmental process.

Another important factor that reinforces the conclusion that normal rating systems are invalid and oppressive is the concept of limits and quotas. Many organizations don't permit raters to make objective evaluations. Some organizations, as well as some individual senior leaders, must approve ratings made by their subordinates even though they might not even know the person being rated. Other organizations assign quotas, usually in percentages, for the number of ratings that may be higher than six, seven or eight.

Problems of the Rating System

The traditional rating process creates more problems, more conflicts, and more lost productivity than any benefit it's designed to gain. Although many inspired leaders, as well as workers, recognize the negative impact of this evaluation process, it tenaciously clings to life.

Workers have no control over the evaluation process. They are its common victims.

Leaders ordinarily have little control over this process, for it exists within the corporation, which has a life of its own to defend. Furthermore, a valid alternative to this judgmental system has not been developed. This system of evaluation has been accepted as better than having no system of evaluation. This standard evaluation process has fundamental weaknesses:

Judgmental Position of the Rater

The person who performs the evaluation and review process is placed into a position of serious judgment. Although this judgment may be justifiably defended by rationalizing the focus on improving the performance of the rated person, it's still a judgmental situation. This judgmental position cannot be totally objective. Even with the best intentions of fair judges, an unbiased evaluation is impossible. Any flaw or error in this process, no matter how small or minor, is still an erroneous judgment. Any misjudgment regarding a person is injustice to the rated person. A small injustice is still injustice.

The rating systems and rating forms are designed as declarations of judgment, not as expressions of opinions. They are designed for workplace conflict. The only way to avoid conflict with this process is to assign everyone a maximum rating, which would erode the value of the system.

Defensive (Vulnerable) Position of the Rated

The rated person is normally allowed to discuss the rating factors the evaluator has judged and assigned. The rated person may even be permitted to include comments on the form to refute or to justify differences of opinion.

From a practical viewpoint, rated persons recognize this review procedure for its ulterior purpose. That ulterior purpose is simply to make the rated person feel he or she is judged objectively. In reality, those who are rated realize the futility of objecting. Even self-confident subordinates usually hesitate to disagree with ratings due to a real or perceived threat of reprisal that ultimately results in quiet resentment. Consequently, true feelings of those ratings of average or less-than-average aren't normally exposed. An astute subordinate also realizes the review discussion is nothing but an administrative formality normally void of sincerity.

Conflict Created by the Rating System

During the rating process, those being rated are aware that they have no control over that process. Any error in judgment, either in the overall assigned rating or with any of the individual factors by the rater, reflects the rater's attitude toward that rated person. It doesn't reflect a fact.

For example, if a rater assigns a rating of seven to a person, in the overall evaluation, that rated person merely believes the rater looks upon that person as a *seven* person. It doesn't mean the rated person considers himself or herself a seven person, since in many cases that rated person doesn't trust or respect the judgment, or the ulterior motives, of that rater. In this situation, only negative results will occur. Those negative results typically include the following:

First, the rated person would assume he or she is identified by the rater as a seven person. Sincere efforts by rated persons to improve themselves usually don't change that first judgment or opinion of personal worth by the rater. Historical evidence shows strong justification for this typical assumption. Once a person is rated as a seven, that person usually continues to be regarded as a seven by raters, regardless of the amount of perceived improvement by the rated person. Often, new or different raters assign ratings based on records in a person's historical file. In many cases senior reviewers will not allow a rater to give a higher rating, based on the rated person's historical file, or based on rating quotas established by the reviewer or the organization.

Second, the rated person may react to the rating that was less than it should have been - in that person's opinion. If a person is judged as a seven, when he or she considers himself or herself an eight or a nine, the reaction may be to drop the perceived performance level to a seven. Why should that person perform at a nine level and only be recognized as a seven level?

Unless the rated person is judged equal to or greater than that person perceives himself or herself to be, the relationship between the rater and the rated person is strained. This reduction in the quality or the confidence of that relationship certainly cannot be expected to result in improved performance and productivity.

In making this analysis, the motivation factors expressed by Abraham Maslow and Frederick Herzberg must be considered. These factors suggest that at a certain level recognition and achievement become more motivational to a person than pay and job security.

Although certainly intended for a positive tool, the current personnel evaluation and review process is, by default, designed to inflict casualties and to incite disharmony in work environments. It interferes with what might otherwise be a positive working relationship. Even at its best, this current process cannot serve a valid purpose - for there are no perfect judges.

Furthermore, there are no perfect people who can perform in such a consistent pattern that the pattern can fairly be assigned an arbitrary number. Only robots might have that capability. A person who's judged as a seven today might be a ten tomorrow. Is that person a seven or a ten?

A worse tragedy is that evaluations are usually performed at the end of a rating period to judge the ratee's past value that cannot be changed for that rated period. A person should be evaluated when either the ratee or the rater feels that a rating will affect performance, confidence, relationships or communications.

There must be an alternative to this oppressive, obsolete and counter-productive process. That alternative will be identified and analyzed next.

A Positive Evaluation Process

A valid and meaningful subordinate evaluation system must accomplish the following goals:

1. Be fair and just
2. Be objective - not judgmental
3. Be mutually participative
4. Offer encouragement - not limitations
5. Improve, not restrict, potential
6. Consider future performance and potential

A progressive evaluation system should also reflect the rater's abilities, confidence and risk that may help motivate subordinates to become more productive and successful through their desire for personal esteem.

A positive and progressive evaluation process must be based upon important relationship factors that must exist in the work environment. This process should consider perceptions, confidence, communications, trust and mutual participation. The process shouldn't be based upon subjective judgments, as in the traditional process.

The evaluation process should be a mutually quantifiable procedure that's determined by open and clear communications by both parties to the process. It may even be necessary to train some subordinates not to fear their superiors in this process, which will serve not only to improve this process, but to improve general communications as well.

This system will consider four rating factors. These factors are the same as the four important words in the Circle of Success:

The confidence level of the person rated

The rated or evaluated person would assign this rating to himself or herself. The rater and the ratee would discuss requirements of the job, qualifications, special expertise, knowledge required and experience. The relationship between those two parties that might influence that rated person's performance should also be considered. That ratee would determine a rating from the traditional scale of one to ten.

The rated person's willingness to assume risk

The rater's confidence in that rated person

These two factors must be considered together by both parties to the evaluation process, for they must be assigned only one mutually agreed rating number from the scale of one to ten. These two factors, mutually considered, analyze the relationship that's essential for an organization to maximize its production capabilities. If those two parties don't agree upon a common rating factor, the two opinions may be averaged to reach that rating factor.

In this process, the person rated must reveal the level of trust that he or she has that the rater will be fair, just and equitable if that rated person gives his or her maximum employeeship efforts. The rater must reveal the confidence level that he or she has in believing that the rated person is dedicated and, in fact, will perform at that employeeship level.

The risk level determined by the rater

The rater assigns this rating factor. This factor would be guided by an overall analysis of all known facts and extenuating circumstances. These would include, at minimum, the following:

Historical performance of the organization
Management support from higher levels
Adequacy of tools and facilities
Overall comfort and security level of the rater
Pending projects or changes
Extent of organizational peer pressure

The rater should consider anything that may cause a question or doubt that might restrict any performance in that workplace. This rating factor would also be assigned a number between one and ten. To complete the process to determine the overall rating, those three factors are multiplied. For example:

Employee confidence		8
	X	
Employee risk and Leader confidence		7
	X	
Leader risk		8
Overall Rating		**448**

A perfect rating is 10 X 10 X 10 = 1000

Improvements by this Rating Process

This relationship rating procedure eliminates the sources of conflict created by those subjective judgmental factors of the traditional method. Low ratings by the traditional method tend to brand the rated person at a certain level which, in effect, becomes the level at which that person is inclined to perform. A person rated as a six realizes that he or she has no control over the judge's decision. In some cases, a rating assigned to a person may increase or decrease simply by the change to a different rater. One rater might determine the rated person to be a seven and a different rater might judge that same person, with that same performance, to be a nine. This judgmental system disqualifies the current evaluation and rating process from being even socially acceptable.

This enhanced relationship evaluation procedure not only removes that conflict and that stigma it also requires, and even forces, open communication between both parties to achieve common perceptions. Each person is aware that the process involves only opinion, and not factual assignment of a fixed number that becomes a label. Each person controls one opinion personally, which helps to decide an opinion that must be formed jointly. Both parties have some control, but neither party is at the judgmental mercy of the other party to determine his or her level of performance.

In effect, this enhanced process is a visual aid to help build worker self-esteem that will be focused on more results to justify and increase that self-esteem. It's also a basis for routine subordinate counseling. To encourage full and open communications, the frequency of this evaluation process should be determined as either person recognizes a change in either of the stated positions.

This rating process is also planned to consider a worker's level of probable productivity as he or she works for and is supported by the overall organization. It's not designed to judge that individual as a person.

An additional advantage will also result from the review phase of this evaluation procedure. Review of the rating should be performed by a senior person in the organization. However, that person should have no authority or control over the factor ratings that are determined by the rater and the person rated. These ratings are self-determined opinions of the professional relationship between those two individuals, this relationship being the cornerstone of productivity. A superior person or the superior organization should have no access to interfere with this relationship other than to advise, counsel or replace an otherwise incompetent or deficient subordinate leader.

That superior must be concerned in two special aspects of this evaluation process:

The superior must determine and analyze changes in the overall average of organizational relationships. Those total numbers may be quantified into one organizational average; or they may be averaged by section, department or by status of individuals. Traditionally, superiors have encouraged or even demanded that rating factors not be inflated. With this new and enhanced rating process, higher rating factors should be interpreted as higher potential for increased productivity and efficiency.

The superior should analyze the rating that the rater assigns himself or herself in the leader risk factor. This factor considers the rater's opinion of his or her risk for the subordinate to maximize his or her potential under the constraints of organizational support and interfacing. That factor also considers the rater's perception of his or her organizational support by that immediate superior. This factor may become the basis for establishing more effective communications at that higher level in the organization.

Summary

The subordinate appraisal, rating and interview process should be an opportunity for leaders and workers to establish mutuality and to focus on success. That success must include the optimum success for the organization and the highest level of success that aspirations will allow subordinates to achieve. The current process not only doesn't allow that to happen, it prevents that from happening.

This weakness in the appraisal and rating process has been recognized, but nothing has been done to improve it. Some efforts have been made, however, they haven't achieved any positive results. For example, different formulas and different factors have been invented to make the process seem different, but the concept of judgment remains the same.

To make the process seem *fair* and *team-like* some organizations even institute programs to allow workers to evaluate, appraise and judge their leaders. It's doubtful that judgements in different directions can result in anything other than restricted communications, for self-defense, and increased conflict. If workers cannot trust leaders to evaluate fairly, why should leaders trust workers to evaluate fairly? Is this scheme to move the judgmental process into an "I can judge you lower than you can judge me" process? Or, maybe it will create leaders who spend more time in a popularity contest and less time acting like leaders concerned with productivity.

The appraisal review process must move beyond the realm of a judgmental contest. It must be designed to serve a positive purpose that creates optimum productivity through more effective communications. This can be achieved by leaders and workers learning mutual perceptions based on words that form the circle of success: confidence, risk, action and results.

11

SOCIAL INFLUENCES

Many organizations have the desire, the ability and the means to become harmonious and productive workplaces. Many organizations have positive and goal-oriented workers who want to succeed and to have a workplace where that success is possible. Many of those workplaces also have competent leaders who are dedicated to productivity and concern for their workers. Even with these high potentials to avoid conflict and to maximize productivity, many organizations never achieve those levels, for social pressures discourage that natural harmony.

Some social pressures exist within the normal workplace, some are created as an extension of the workplace and others have no direct relationship to the workplace. Yet, all contribute to the attitudes, values, despair, opinions, judgments and decisions of all members of a workplace. The influences persuade, convince, entice or otherwise encourage members of a workplace to take actions or make decisions that they would not ordinarily make if they were left to their own perceptions. Without the influence of these factors, conflict in the workplace would be an anomaly. The most important of these influences include:

- Peer Pressure

195

- Governmental Regulations
- Political Rhetoric
- Social Leadership Distrust
- Attorney Enticement
- Welfare Alternatives
- Organized Labor

Peer Pressure

Peer pressure is the most direct, dynamic and forceful influence that contributes to conflict in a workplace. Although some peer pressure may have positive influences in special situations, most peer pressure is designed for negative consequences. These negative consequences ordinarily result in conflict, for that negative pressure forces workers into employee acquiescence that widens the conflict zone.

The powerful influence of peer pressure has been partially hidden and obscured in the work environment. It hasn't been open and blatant to expose itself as a routine workplace problem that must be solved. An explanation is necessary to understand the hidden nature of peer pressure.

It's important to remember that peer pressure routinely is regarded as a force or a condition that affects young children and teenagers. Peer pressure begins and is learned at an early age, as soon as children understand that they have control over others by withholding their toys or by withholding their playtime from other children who don't comply with their demands. This early peer pressure begins with controlling comments such as:

"If you don't stop that, I won't let you play with my train - doll, car, etc."

"I'm not going to play with you anymore, if you don't play

196

fair."

"If you don't stop that, I'm going to tell your dad."

These are typical comments from young children whose major concerns are playing, toys and avoiding mean adults.

Eventually, peer pressure evolves into the teenage years. Although the pressure is the same, tactics are somewhat different for it begins to focus on belonging, esteem and intelligence. The desire to be normal, during the teenage years, becomes the source of greatest vulnerability. To attack that vulnerability, peer pressure often uses comments similar to these:

"What are you doing that for, Stupid?"

"That's a dumb-looking pair of shoes you have on."

"You mean your parents won't let you do that?"

"Is studying all you ever do?"

"We would ask you to go with us, but we plan to drink a little and have some real fun."

These typical teenage tactics are designed to threaten separation and isolation to force another to conform to the ideologies of a reference group. At this stage of one's life, teenagers are usually considered as a single reference group, consequently, that pressure is basically uniform and consistent.

When the teenage years pass and one becomes a working adult, does peer pressure disappear? Although it ceases to be a topic of major concern (everyone is still focused on teenage peer pressure) it takes on a new face with even more power than teenage peer pressure. Adult peer pressure becomes even more devastating than teenage peer pressure, for it tends to influence one's financial and emotional status.

Adult peer pressure wears many masks to camouflage itself, it rarely shows itself. Those masks include innuendo, suggestions, understandings, consensus, gestures and facial expressions. Adult peer pressure rarely exposes itself to allow itself to be defeated. It remains safely on the fringes of subtlety. Adult peer pressure has grown up; it knows how to protect itself. Typical adult peer pressure comments in the workplace include:

"What are you doing that for?"

"Are you trying to make us look bad?"

"No one really appreciates what you are doing."

"You did that much today! Why?"

"Are you trying to get promoted, or something?"

"You will just burn yourself out!"

"Are you trying to brown-nose the boss?"

These are typical adult peer pressure comments designed to force someone to be less productive or less cooperative than a person ordinarily would be. These are the comments that really mean, "You are doing more than your fellow workers to improve yourself to develop a career and to make a major contribution in life; and we don't like that. If you don't accept our standards we might not associate with (play with) you again."

Adult peer pressure also has a more insidious face than does teenage peer pressure or childhood peer pressure. Those two novices require spoken words and direct comments. Adult peer pressure may be used without spoken words. The worst of adult peer pressure is exercised by innuendo, gestures and acceptance of understood standards. Experiments by Soloman Asch proved that under controlled conditions people may be influenced to change their minds of a correct decision when they feel that that decision doesn't match the decision of the majority. This study concerned a simple experiment of determining the length of lines.

How does workplace peer pressure contribute to workplace conflict? Ordinarily, workplace peer pressure is designed for two negative purposes. One is to encourage fellow workers not to be overly productive. Obvious productivity might discredit other workers or force them also to become more productive. This is probably the major basis for the conclusion that the level of productivity by American workers is only fifty percent of its potential. The second purpose is to maintain the traditional antithesis between the values of leaders and the values of workers. In either case, continued workplace conflict is the natural result.

Governmental Regulations

Governmental regulations, policies, and guidelines are designed to reflect ideas and concepts of the free choice of a democratic society to protect and enhance that society. This grandiose ideal is not always a matter of practice. Often, governmental control is initiated and enforced as a result of pressure, demands, or desires of special interest groups that don't necessarily reflect a benefit or a gain for society.

These actions often occur, instead, for those special interests, and for public officials focused on elections. The lack of valid economic concerns by policy-makers often creates conflict in work environments that wouldn't otherwise have that conflict.

An example of imposed conflict is demonstrated by the governmental policy that workplaces be racially mixed to reflect the racial structure of a community. Although socially and morally proper, this policy could have negative consequences; for equal opportunity doesn't necessarily create equal results and achievements. Furthermore, if a workplace doesn't function at its highest potential, society fails to create a broader base of opportunities for those it claims to protect.

Some serious questions must be considered regarding the

effects of forced mixing simply to proclaim that everyone in our society has equal opportunities. These important questions include:

If businesses aren't allowed to hire the most competent workers, regardless of race or ethnic origin, can those businesses maximize productivity and competition to create more jobs and opportunities for more people?

If businesses aren't allowed to function as businesses to maximize productivity that will create more jobs and opportunities, will the social problem of discrimination ever be solved?

Will an artificially integrated workplace ever avoid the conflict that restricts productivity? Shouldn't the workplace be integrated under more natural conditions, such as the need for productivity and preparation of workers?

Can a minority person who gets a job through forced integration ever develop the esteem he or she must have feel successful? Or, will that person be a source of conflict by continued self-justification?

Should the workplace be a place for building the economic strength of a country to provide opportunities for everyone, or should the workplace be used by society as a tool for expedient social manipulation?

Another example that represents a similar set of questions concerns the extra consideration and the extra protection that government gives to persons classified as disabled. Again, this is also a socially acceptable and altruistic gesture to care for persons who need special help. This conforms to American religious values and idealism. It doesn't, however, conform to the concept of a workplace as a place for economic opportunity and strength of a country.

Framers of governmental rules or policies that place special protection for select groups of people in the job market might handicap others in the job market; and, might even reduce opportunities in the job market. Consider the following questions, where specialized hiring is enforced to comply with governmental policies:

Will people be replaced with technology to avoid the vulnerable position of frivolous accusations and litigation? Each litigation may cost thousands of dollars, which itself prevents other workers from being hired.

If government and society restrict the ability of businesses to make business decisions, should businesses remain in this country to create opportunities that are not appreciated? Shouldn't the selection of workers, who leaders feel will make the greatest contribution to productivity, profit, and more opportunities for citizens be an accountable business decision?

During times of less than full employment, when the unemployment rate is high, what happens to other people who need jobs but cannot find them, because those jobs are filled with protected workers? Regardless of the positive and supportive rhetoric, business will be forced to hire less qualified workers to protect themselves against expensive litigation. Will those who are hired always be the best to help enlarge the economic opportunities for others?

Is special protection for select groups in a free and democratic society in the best interests of that society? Can conflict ever be avoided where some have special consideration? Wouldn't it be more reasonable to develop a society, and an economy, that would require the inclusion of those special groups as part of the economic process, through demand? That demand must be created through productivity.

From an economic perspective, perhaps the business of business and the business of social manipulation should be separated so that each might have a more pristine perspective and each might make more progress. A 'good' society cannot exist without a strong economic society; and a strong economic society might not exist without a 'good' society. If these are artificially mixed through force, and not by growing economic opportunity and requirements, conflict is inevitable, and worse economic and social disasters are likely to occur.

Similar socially-oriented policies have been tried in other countries, and they haven't fared well. Should we expect to do any better under a similar concept simply because we are *good religious people?*

A timely question might be, "Who makes these vague laws and regulations that require money, time, and litigation to resolve, anyway?" Every law relating to social engineering and special rights is never specific. Could it be the same people who make the laws, mostly attorneys, are the only real winners in that litigation process? Plaintiffs and defendants in these cases both usually lose something in the litigation process, regardless of who actually wins. Workplace conflict, as well as social conflict continues to be perpetuated in this artificial process.

Political Rhetoric

Elected officials, or those persons seeking elected positions, make speeches and issue statements to convince people they are supporting their interests. The purpose for these statements is to gain votes, or to gain favor. The result of many of those statements is to enlarge the zone of conflict between leaders and workers.

An example of rhetorical abuse that perpetuates workplace conflict by alienating workplace interests concerns the subject of executive pay and privileges. Politicians often give speeches about the moral inequity and the unfairness for top company executives to receive high salaries and special privileges. Although this might be a valid charge, and totally true; nevertheless, the only result from those rhetorical proclamations is to convince workers to alienate themselves from leaders, since leaders are portrayed only as greedy and insensitive. Exceptions aren't allowed for those leaders who aren't greedy and insensitive. Political rhetoric isn't likely to have any real influence on executive salaries.

Another example of rhetorical abuse is made by those same people, in the presence of a leadership group, who bemoan the lack of skilled workers. Suddenly those exploited workers who were staunchly defended by the politician who will change the world in their favor now become the cause of all the world's economic problems. The rhetorical orator attempts to convince leaders that he or she will save their companies by helping them to develop a better workforce, since most workers are now unskilled and unmotivated.

Society, including public leaders in society, doesn't encourage mutual harmony, trust, and cooperation in the workplace. Instead, their rhetoric continues to maintain a large conflict zone in most work environments. A mutually harmonious, cooperative, and productive work environment would eliminate a source of special interest votes for many self-serving politicians.

Peter Drucker, in his foreward to C. Northgate Parkinson's book, *Communicate,* makes a pertinent statement regarding society's approach toward business:

"And so a public, which by no means shares the beliefs of the enemies of business, goes along with their proposed policies and laws simply because it lacks the understanding to oppose what in the long run then always turns out to be detrimental to the very public that supports - or at least accepts - the laws and regulations and measures proposed by the enemies of business."

Although some individual business leaders might be less than honorable, greedy, and insensitive, business nevertheless serves a positive and worthwhile purpose. Actions by society, including negative rhetoric, that limit or restrict the ability of business to perform its economic function create results detrimental to the society it's designed to serve.

Social Leadership Distrust

Productivity, whether in social environments or work environments, requires confidence, trust, and mutual cooperation toward a common goal. There's a strong decline in the level of confidence and trust that ordinary people in society have toward their leaders. There's a forgone conclusion among many in society that it doesn't matter who's elected to a leadership position, for that person will be incompetent, incapable, elitist, and maybe even selfish once that desired position is attained. Suddenly the person who was promising to do great things to change the world now has only a briefcase full of excuses to explain why those things cannot be done.

Those excuses usually have two bases. First, the other political party is the obstacle. Secondly, more money is needed to solve the problem. Perhaps if one party could be annihilated and enough money printed, our country would no longer have any problems. Or, is it just possible that answers to our social problems might be based upon more fundamental concepts, such as: ideas, honesty, action, total interest, competency, and just taking a first step in the right direction?

Regardless of the base of our social problems, or the possible answers to these problems, social leadership to correct those problems remains frustrated and obviously inadequate. How does this contribute to conflict in the normal work environment? Simply, a feeling of distrust of leadership, any leadership, prevails in our society.

Since there are leaders in most work environments, that

leadership is included in the general consensus of incompetent and inadequate leadership. This general lack of distrust tends to create defensive leaders and insecure workers. The modern term given to describe these insecure workers is 'alienated' workers. The natural result is a wider zone of conflict.

Attorney Enticement

A major condition that's necessary for productivity and harmony in a workplace is the cooperation and trust between workers and leaders. A rising trend is taking place that threatens to destroy that essential cooperation and trust. This negative trend is caused by a combination of some over-zealous attorneys and susceptible workers.

Many attorneys now advertise on television, radio, and written media for workers to file lawsuits against their employers for perceived rights and injustices. They promise potential clients in their media persuasion that they will "get everything you deserve" if they file a claim. Many of these emotional pressure tactics are too powerful for a marginal and susceptible person to resist.

The most de-motivational area of questionable litigation concerns claims for workers compensation for on-the-job injuries. Although there's an established system to compensate injured workers, with even training and rehabilitation programs included, many injured workers are enticed by pressure advertising to file lawsuits for larger lump-sum settlements.

Attorneys share in the lump-sum proceeds, and at no risk to themselves. There are such restrictions in this process against management's rights that these lump-sum payments are often required even when all parties to the litigation suspect or know that the claim is, in fact, false.

Occasionally, an inspired manager or the insurance company will hire private sources to prove the claimant is committing fraud by faking an injury. This is usually done with photographs and film of the claimant performing a physical act that he or she claims he or she cannot do. Even when the claim is proved false, however, the claimant or the initiating attorney ordinarily are not charged with fraud or conspiracy for those activities. In effect, this effort is almost risk free by both the attorney and the faking worker.

Notwithstanding the possible unlawful activities of this process, this system creates negative environments in many workplaces that restrict trust and mutual cooperation for leaders and workers. Leaders often show their apprehension of the possibility of fraudulent or nuisance claims against them, in which case they are usually defenseless, and become reluctant to allow some workers to work within their full range of independent capability. From a practical standpoint, many leaders feel they must watch their workers more closely to identify any potential indications that the worker cannot be trusted.

This close supervision becomes conflict encroachment into the conflict zone. The leader is not free to concentrate on more progressive things in the organization that will allow more productivity, esteem, and harmony. The worker, who is not allowed to work within his or her full range of potential feels limited and restricted. Neither is able to reach his or her goals.

Furthermore, a worse tragedy may occur that creates more distrust and conflict. Other workers who understand the process tend to become frustrated and apprehensive. Many dedicated and loyal workers resent the fraudulent activities of their peers, and are apprehensive about the possible retaliation by their leaders.

This problem of over-zealous litigation enticed by strong attorney advertising is a rapidly growing menace that threatens even worse damage in the modern workplace. Clearly, those who are injured on-the-job deserve just compensation in accordance with rules that were intended for that purpose. These honest situations don't cause the problem. The menace is the growing abuse, false claims, and nothing less than actual fraud that has little defense against its occurrence.

What might correct this problem that encourages ambivalence and distrust that leads to continued conflict in the workplace? Probably nothing, since that's not the politically correct approach. Furthermore, business and industry would be charged as unfair if they suggested injured workers shouldn't be compensated for their injuries; which would most likely be the social interpretation of their actions.

Consequently, business leaders have no socially correct course of action to initiate changes. Policy makers have no financial incentive to make corrective changes, since policy makers are usually those same attorneys, or their peers and associates, who profit from those policies. Without a combined effort by business and society correction to this growing pattern of invalid claims, without a practical defense to question their validity, will probably not occur.

The conflict this problem creates is subtle, however, it continues to grow like an amoeba gone wild. Its tentacles reach into all vulnerable areas of society to create hesitancy and ambivalence that restrict people from open, motivated, and harmonious actions.

If this trend of attorney enticement continues to grow it wouldn't be unrealistic to imagine the following advertisement in the near future:

ARE YOU HAVING PROBLEMS WITH YOUR PARENTS OR YOUR GRANDPARENTS? ARE THEY HASSLING YOU AND TRYING TO TELL YOU WHAT TO DO? THIS IS NOT RIGHT! YOU DESERVE BETTER TREATMENT THAN THAT! CALL HONEST SMILEY SNIVELY TODAY AND HE WILL GET YOU WHAT YOU DESERVE IN JUST COMPENSATION. YOU OWE NOTHING UNLESS HONEST SMILEY COLLECTS FOR YOU. (Honest Smiley Snively is a fictitious name, not based upon or intended to describe any real person.)

To begin a corrective adjustment in social attitudes toward business and industry, business must become more active rhetorically to inform citizens of the real purpose for business and the real advantages society gains by supporting business. Presently, most business leaders are simply trying to ameliorate the damage by avoiding what could be real social interaction and influence. In other words, their normal tactics are defensive rather than offensive.

If business is to fulfill its economic development and expansion role to create more social opportunities, business leaders must become more aggressive to explain their purpose and value to society. If those leaders refuse this obligation, other opportunists will continue to use their silence as an opportunity for personal self-interests.

Welfare Alternatives

Welfare systems have been a long tradition in this country. Even in the early 1800s survival systems were improvised to care for the sick, elderly, cast-offs, and those who were temporarily unemployed. This concept was identified as relief, with an alternative of the concept of a poorhouse. Poorhouses really existed where desperate people could go for temporary relief.

People who accepted relief, or went to those poorhouses, did so from desperation, not from the choice of an alternative lifestyle. The work ethic was strong at that time and able-bodied people who could find jobs went to work as soon as they could. History indicates those people were too independent and had too much pride to rely on others for their normal existence.

Later, between the two world wars, there was a great depression. During this period there was relief, which included the concept of soup lines. Even during this traumatic period in history people still had a high work ethic and preferred to find a job, no matter how lowly or demeaning, to earn their own way and to provide for their families.

A great political event occurred in the 1960s. Poverty was discovered in the United States. In a moment of Divine inspiration, political forces, particularly two presidential administrations, decided to make that new discovery a political cause. One of those presidents even decided to wipe out poverty, an accomplishment no other president or no other leader in history had ever done. This was the beginning of a 'Great Society' where everyone would be *taken care of*. The unspoken implication was that, "You are no longer really responsible for your actions or your success. The government will take care of you, if you really can't do it yourself."

Since that period in our history, relief or welfare assistance hasn't been considered as help or assistance; it became regarded as a *right* by many people. As a *right*, it became a logical and rational alternative to accepting undesirable jobs. With normal welfare assistance as a logical alternative people now have more lifestyle choices, which include:

1. To improve one's abilities and skills by training

2. To complete higher education

3. To find an entry level job to begin a career

4. To rely on customary family support

5. To rely on governmental support

These choices are clear alternatives in our society. Each person decides, either actively or passively, from this list.

The choice of governmental support as an alternative lifestyle encourages some vulnerable people to make that choice rather than choosing to contribute to national productivity. Let's consider an example of this alternative choice and how it contributes to workplace conflict. For this example we will consider Judith, who works as a desk clerk in a laundry office:

Judith lives with her boyfriend, Robert, and her four year old daughter, Amanda. She's divorced from Amanda's father, who abandoned them two years ago. She has been working at Classic Cleaners for six months, earning a minimum wage. She quit school in the tenth grade, so she never developed enough skills for a good career. Most potential employers will not even give her an application form for a job, since she didn't finish high school. She felt fortunate when Classic Cleaners hired her as a desk clerk.

After six months at that job, however, Judith began to question herself about the logic of working at a minimum wage job. She knew she would never have a good job that would provide enough money for her needs, and enough esteem for her to feel self-respect and pride. Judith didn't have to pay for a baby-sitter because her mother, who lived only five blocks from Judith, usually kept Amanda while Judith worked. Her mother's help, however, still didn't allow Judith's income to pay all her expenses.

Judith learned from two of her friends that she could get free money from the government, since she had a young daughter and she didn't have a husband to provide them with family support. Her friends also told Judith there were other benefits such as: free medical care, food stamps, lower-cost housing, and unlimited training if she didn't find a job she liked. The idea that these three friends could have more time together to have fun also appealed to Judith.

Judith really didn't want to take that approach, for she had always been taught that something should be earned; 'you shouldn't ask for a free handout if you're able to work for yourself.' She knew she could work. At this time she didn't even have a good reason to quit her job.

During the next month, Judith began to be bothered by little events on the job that hadn't bothered her before. Customers seemed to be more demanding, her co-workers seemed to become more belligerent, and her boss was becoming more uncooperative. He even told her to do some things that she felt weren't part of her job. She felt it wasn't right that she should tolerate all this unfair harassment.

She told her complaining customers she was doing the best she could to get their clothes returned on time, and that she "can't do anything about it." She began to tell her co-workers, "Just leave me alone, and mind your own business." She even told her boss, on two occasions, "Why do you always tell me to do everything? There are other people who work here besides myself, and they usually just stand around doing nothing."

Her boss, after two more months of trying to let Judith correct her attitude problem that was causing conflict with other workers, as well as loss of the loyalty of some good customers, decided to counsel Judith about her problem. He was a patient and caring boss, but he had seen enough to understand Judith was her own worst problem. He asked Judith to come into his office so they could "talk."

Judith's boss explained to Judith that her attitude had changed recently, and it was causing conflict in the plant as well as loss of some good customers. He asked Judith, "Do you have any problems that might be causing this that I might help you with?"

Judith answered, "Most of the customers are stupid; and your other workers are just lazy and concerned only about themselves. That's just the way they are. Now you're hassling me too. Why don't you take care of the real problems instead of blaming me?"

Her boss answered, "Judith, I've been watching this problem grow for the past two months. I have basically the same customers that I've had for years, and most of my workers have been with me for a long time. I'm aware of their dedication and performance. The situation that we're discussing now is your problem, not problems of other people. Can we talk about the real issue so that we might find a way to correct it?"

Judith instantly replied, "Well, if that's the attitude you are going to take; if you're going to believe those other people instead of me, you can just take this job and shove it. I don't need it enough to put up with this hassle."

Why did Judith develop her attitude problem that created conflict in her work environment? She knew she could choose an alternative lifestyle that required less work, and allowed more free time to have fun with her friends. Her job and her potential career became obstacles to her immediate short-sighed and short-planned desires. Those obstacles became a source of conflict.

This isn't an extreme example of the role welfare policies play in our society. This is a typical example of the real choices that real people make every day.

This lifestyle alternative causes weak productivity from the conflict that it creates in a workplace; but that's minor compared to the real tragedy it creates. The major tragedy for those individuals, and for society, is that it entices vulnerable people who might otherwise try to become successful actively to choose to be failures.

This problem must be solved by approaching it from two perspectives. First, public assistance must be changed from the concept of a permanent alternative lifestyle to the concept of short-term assistance to fulfill unexpected and critical needs. Secondly, members of lower cultures who don't understand the success process must be taught those simple steps, including the confidence that those success steps really are simple. They must not be allowed a lifestyle alternative that destroys the motivation to consider that simple process.

Labor Organizations

Ordinarily there are three basic opinions toward labor organizations, usually referred to as unions. These include:

1. They are obstacles that reduce productivity.
2. They are necessary to protect workers.
3. They once served a good purpose, but now they are useless and serve no purpose.

The first two opinions regarding unions normally aren't opinions. For many people they are firm value beliefs that must be protected and defended. The first point of view is usually that of management, and the second point of view is that of unions and many of their members, especially members with a family history of union membership and union support, their culture. The third viewpoint is usually shared by those who have no strong beliefs in either opinion. The purpose for identifying organized labor as a source of workplace conflict is not to express a value judgment regarding the need or the purpose for unions. All three viewpoints expressed above are probably valid for each organizations' purpose.

Unions do restrict effective productivity in many business organizations, sometimes to the extent of causing businesses to fail. Some workers do need protection from those despotic, tyrannical, and insensitive leaders who still exist within a more understanding leadership world. Unions did, in fact, serve a clearly worthwhile purpose during the inception of labor organizations. That need, to eliminate forced labor sweat shops, was the basis for the formation of organized labor.

This analysis is to recognize the impact organized labor influence sometimes has upon the harmony, or conflict, in the work environment; and to determine how that influence negatively affects the success aspirations of individual workers, especially those who are members. Although unions may serve a worthwhile purpose for workers as a group, they often create more conflict, frustration, despair, and failure to workers as individuals.

Labor organizations are simply business organizations that struggle for survival as any other business organization that's organized to provide income and profit to its owners. To survive, and to continue the revenue base, unions must have members. For that revenue base unions must provide something its members interpret as having value.

This interpreted value members receive in return for their membership dues includes protection, justice, and more benefits and security. These are the things that Maslow, in his motivation theory, classifies as the lower order physiological needs. Herzberg's Two-Factor theory identifies these things as hygiene factors, not motivators. Pay, benefits, job security, fair supervision, and good working conditions are normal expectations in a work environment. For labor organizations to survive they must convince their members, and society, that workers are cheated and unfairly treated by business and industrial leaders. They focus on these physiological and safety needs to create that conflict, for those needs are more visible and interpretable than the higher needs. Those higher needs of esteem, which are really the basis of worker satisfaction, are never allowed to be exposed by labor leaders. They cannot reasonably promise members they can have more esteem by negotiating and striking, if necessary. The exception might be that the power they exhibit is a display of group influence and esteem   .

Interpretation of these two recognized motivation theories suggests that labor organizations keep the emphasis of their members, and workers generally, on the non-motivational needs. That focus is directed toward truth, justice, fair-play, honor, security, and defending a polarized position rather than on each worker's personal success plan. If a worker's concerns are kept focused on organized labor's goals and ideologies, then that worker cannot rise above those ideologies to understand the concept of allowing himself or herself to become motivated to strive for real personal goals and real success. Without this motivation to develop a valid personal success plan, members' concerns remain focused on those hygiene factors emphasized by their union leaders.

Labor, in effect, discourages individualism which doesn't allow members to see or to understand how to become self-motivated to achieve real individual success. Too many successful workers would eliminate the perceived need for union organizations. This explains the concept of labor organizations as an obstacle to personal motivation, which ultimately evolves into perpetual workplace conflict. Continued conflict makes personal success and personal esteem seem further removed from possibility and reality. The circle of despair and conflict continues.

This conflict is based on the assumption that one's success is determined by the generosity of leaders in the work environment.

Real success is determined by one's individual efforts to develop a personal success plan. That success plan might not even be related to one's current workplace. Greater success usually comes from maintaining good work habits while improving one's knowledge and qualifications for a different job. A bigger pay raise, alone, is not success. Sometimes it's just an anchor to drag down a lost road.

For example, a person might be working as an assembly-line worker in a manufacturing plant, but that worker might have a success plan to become a certified public accountant. In this example, union activities might convince this worker that the success of the union is more important than becoming an accountant. Workplace conflict would be perpetuated, for the worker would be convinced the workplace caused his or her failure to become successful.

Summary

These social influences on workplace harmony haven't been identified and discussed necessarily to be critical or judgmental, or to offer grandiose answers. Instead, they have been recognized and discussed to demonstrate that workplace conflict is often caused by factors outside the workplace that suffers from that conflict.

Even when work environments are staffed with competent leaders and motivated workers many of these social influences don't allow those positive factors to merge into harmonious relationships that create effective productivity. Negative social influences don't keep their tentacles removed from the workplace, especially since most workplaces are only small representations of a broader society that reflect the values and beliefs of society.

Although these negative social influences cannot be solved within the narrow confines of a normal workplace they must, nevertheless, be addressed within each workplace. In this process leaders must insure workers understand how to develop a success plan, and how these negative social influences might affect those success plans.

That expression of concern for workers might help to eliminate the natural conflict that results from those negative social influences. To ignore these negative influences will never allow leaders and workers to achieve the level of harmony and success in their workplaces they all desire.

12

RESOLVING WORKPLACE CONFLICT

It's easy to realize from all the problems, ideologies, differences of opinion, differences of objectives, and differences of goals in a work environment, that the avoidance of conflict seems impossible. Apparently, this has been the conclusion for many generations of leaders and workers, for workplace conflict exists in most work environments as merely another part of that environment.

Most leaders discuss that conflict, but rarely do they really try to eliminate or reduce it. When they make attempts to reduce conflict, those attempts are normally aimed at morale, which is the wrong target. Perhaps they cannot aim toward the right target, conflict, because they haven't been given proper weapons that may be used to aim at that vague target.

Enough information has been given in this book to make that target more visible and less vague. Workplace conflict has been clearly identified and described. Furthermore, specific causes of that conflict have also been revealed. With this understanding of workplace conflict, it's now time to develop a clear and effective strategy to eliminate that lingering problem that's been an accepted part of most normal work environments.

217

Workplace conflict has, heretofore, been accepted as a normal part of the work environment, not because it's enjoyed, but because it's been accepted as 'coming with the territory' in those relationships between leaders and workers.

Part of that coming with the territory concept includes a new word which suggests the despair of that concept. This new word is alienation. Since leaders haven't determined how to motivate workers to be interested, dedicated, and more productive, it's become fashionable for leaders to assume workers have become alienated. This suggests workers are alienated from loyalties and productivity concerns.

This might be somewhat true. However, a worse pattern of alienation has been created for workers by allowing workplace conflict to continue. For workers, this alienation includes:

Alienation of self-awareness

Alienation of self-respect

Alienation of rational thinking

Alienation of goals

Alienation of need or motivator influences

Alienation of hope

Alienation of a meaningful life

Alienation of dreams

Leaders ordinarily are concerned with trying to find motivation techniques that will reduce the alienation workers have toward work and productivity concerns. Perhaps that workplace alienation might more easily be eliminated by removing the alienation that has been forced upon workers toward themselves.

That strategy to eliminate workplace conflict has five areas of consideration. These include:

218

Clear functions of authority and responsibility
A new leadership style - supportive leadership
Understanding and use of employeeship
Individual success planning
Acknowledgment of negative social pressures

Each of these considerations will be discussed, individually, below.

Authority and Responsibility

Frustration, confusion, blame, and discomfort often occur when clear limits of authority, responsibility, and decision-making aren't established in an organization. This concept is suggested by Tannenbaum and Schmidt's Continuum of Leadership Theory. Although this theory doesn't show the conflict factor in the leadership process, it does recognize there is a different range, a continuum, in the assignment and acceptance of authority and decision-making in different leadership styles. When authorities and responsibilities aren't clearly assigned and understood, conflict is the natural order.

Many workplaces assign specific duties to workers instead of assigning geographical or functional areas of responsibility. Specific duties ordinarily suggest repetitious tasks, not authority and decision-making. An unskilled or a semi-skilled worker is rarely told, or understands, the clear limits of authority that accompany those duties. Ordinarily the leader assumes the worker understands when he or she should make necessary decisions. The worker, on the other hand, assumes he or she hasn't been given that decision-making authority.

The uncertainty of this typical situation automatically and consistently creates conflict, for the worker is hesitant to make decisions; and the leader believes the worker is stupid, incompetent, lazy, or disinterested. This attitude by the leader, expressed by direct comment or innuendo, causes the worker to become defensive and less confident in his or her abilities.

A major complaint, possibly the major complaint by business leaders today, is that the public education system is failing to provide business and industry with qualified entry level workers. Is this really a valid conclusion, or are those business leaders failing to really allow those workers to demonstrate they are more capable? Perhaps that self-defensive conclusion by leaders creates a vicious circle of worker alienation.

Why should workers feel an integral part of the workforce if they know their leaders have already concluded they aren't qualified to be part of the normal workforce? A valid conclusion that workers aren't prepared to make decisions cannot be validated until leaders allow those workers *the clear and defined opportunity to make those decisions.*

To develop a work atmosphere that permits natural harmony and productivity, each subordinate in that work environment must know his or her duties in that workplace. Knowledge of those duties doesn't mean simply to understand the physical requirement of the task; it also means to understand decision-making and the limits of that decision-making to fully perform that task.

Three things are critical in clearly assigning responsible tasks. These are:

Each person must understand the concepts of the success circle described in Chapter Nine.

The worker must be trained and qualified, or be given time to learn the job.

Leaders and workers must understand the concepts of errors and mistakes described in Chapter Six.

These three basics are critical to help leaders and workers develop confidence and trust in each other, so they may not be distracted from the task of developing and maintaining productivity. If leaders and workers are distracted by personality and emotional and confidence factors they will have less time to do the task that's the primary purpose for their workplace existence. That task is to produce something that results in effective profit.

A worker who doesn't know the full scope of his or her job, including the level of decision-making permitted in that job, cannot fulfill the full scope of that job. Leaders must insure workers know the full content of their jobs, including the limit of decision-making to perform that job. This condition is assuming, of course, the leader is not an autocratic leader who doesn't trust anyone, or who doesn't want to share the 'glory' of decision-making in his or her organization. This implication of leadership styles will be discussed next.

Leadership

A leader's leadership style directly contributes to the level of harmony or conflict that determines cooperation and productivity in an organization. Traditional leadership styles were identified in Chapter Three. In summary, these three styles have the following characteristics:

The Autocratic Leadership Style

The autocratic leader acts under the concepts of McGregor's Theory X leadership approach. This approach emphasizes that workers must be driven and coerced to perform, for they are lazy and cannot be trusted with responsibility. The autocratic leader doesn't share decision-making with workers, thereby disallowing those workers to anticipate meaningful work, recognition, or a feeling of personal achievement.

Although an autocratic leader might maintain effective

productivity, that productivity assumes workers are merely workplace tools, not people. Consequently, an autocratic leader naturally creates alienation and conflict. This idea is not to suggest an autocratic leader is a 'bad' person. This conclusion is simply to acknowledge that while acting as an autocratic leader, that person creates conflict.

The Human Relations Leadership Style

The human relations style takes a different approach. Human relations leaders (also called democratic leaders) are guided by the concepts of McGregor's Theory Y approach. Theory Y assumes workers are guided to work naturally by their desire for meaningful work, achievement, recognition, pride, and recognition. In this approach the human relations leader tries to include workers in the meaningful work process, which includes responsibility and decision-making.

If the human relations leader is competent, and is supported by his or her superiors, that workplace will tend to have less conflict than a workplace led by an autocratic leader. Of course, this situation is not certain; for the abilities, values, beliefs, and expectations of workers in that workplace also play major roles in determining the level of conflict.

The Laissez-Faire Leadership Style

This style could more appropriately be defined as an abdication of leadership than as a real leadership style. A leader who functions under this concept isn't interested in the responsibilities and the rewards of leadership. This leader is either too cowardly to be a leader or doesn't have enough authority to be a leader. Often, this leader is more interested in doing tasks personally than in leading to insure those tasks are done. Many leaders even recognize their inability to confidently direct workers, so they avoid that uncomfortable position.

Any avoidance to exercise leadership by a person who occupies a formal leadership position suggests laissez-faire leadership. In that situation, workers are left to function without coordinated and confident productivity plans. Although free to perform as they wish, this lack of coordinated direction tends to create continuing conflict among workers.

These descriptions of leadership styles suggest conflict has good reasons to exist in organizations led by a leader who functions under either of those traditional styles. The question of productivity versus human concerns, justice, and equity prevail under either of these conditions.

To eliminate or reduce these conditions that contribute directly to workplace conflict, perhaps a new leadership style should be considered. This new leadership style should be programed and designed to recognize and to give equal and fair emphasis to the needs of productivity in the workplace, and to the needs of the worker as a person. The human relations style attempts to recognize these needs, somewhat, but that emphasis remains focused on encouraging and motivating workers to concentrate on company goals; not the personal goals of the workers.

The hypocrisy of traditional human relations leadership is that it tries to convince workers that goals of workers should be the same as the goals of the company. A harmonious leadership style must ordinarily recognize those goals as separate goals. This new style should be identified and conceptualized as 'supportive leadership,' which will be described next.

Supportive Leadership

Although at this time supportive leadership doesn't exist as a recognized style, some facets of supportive leadership exist in many organizations. The military services are probably closer to a supportive leadership style than most other organizations; and they are probably closer to supportive leadership than they, themselves, realize. Although the military services are considered to be *military,* they are also equally *human.* This concept of supportive leadership is, in large part, based on those ideals.

To define supportive leadership, there must be a clear conceptual statement. This statement that defines supportive leadership is:

> Supportive leadership is that style of leadership that emphasizes and supports the goals of the company; and, at the same time, encourages and supports the goals of workers that may or may not be the same goals of the company. Supportive leaders also teach workers how to define those personal goals for themselves and how to develop a success plan to reach those goals.

A supportive leader would fulfill the following requirements:

- Train subordinates in success planning principles.

- Assist subordinates in determining realistic success goals.

- Maintain formal records of subordinates' self-generated and self-determined progress.

- Remove external demotivators from the work environment.

- Work against those obstacles to personal employee success.

- Recognize and encourage personal esteem for each

person in the organization.

- Insure subordinate appraisal and rating systems are fair, equitable, just, and not simply judgmental.

- Understand that goals of the organization may not be the personal goals of workers.

- Strive to achieve a relationship factor of 1000 for the organization, as explained in Chapter Ten.

- Quickly remove any subordinate who refuses to learn or practice good employeeship (acquiescence.)

- Quickly remove any leader who refuses to learn or practice effective leadership (acquiescence or encroachment.)

- Train superior leaders in supportive leadership.

- Never be satisfied or complacent with the established average organization. Refuse mediocrity.

These supportive leadership functions might seem similar to those of the democratic, or human relations, leadership style. There are significant differences. The supportive leader acknowledges that worker goals aren't synonymous with company goals, although they could be the same, depending upon the subordinate. The leader provides active training and guidance not directly related to company productivity.

The supportive leader doesn't try to motivate by manipulation; but instead, removes demotivators to allow subordinates to develop their natural motivation. These leaders also assist subordinates to overcome other success obstacles.

Finally, the supportive leader expects a higher level of involvement, concern, and employeeship. Subordinate leaders, as well, must be more prepared to provide supportive leadership. This leadership style demands higher professionalism in the workplace. In return, the supportive leader reciprocates by providing inspiration, freedom, esteem, and guidance to help each subordinate reach his or her highest possible success goals. Increased esteem encourages a person's personality and perceptions to reject the need for defensive conflict.

Employeeship

Employeeship is a major factor often not identified as a contributor to workplace harmony that permits effective productivity. That employee factor is recognized, but that recognition usually considers only a narrow view of workers' skills or motivations. In this narrow view, workers who help create conflict in the workplace are regarded as merely unskilled or unmotivated. Or, they might be regarded as lacking a good work ethic. Ordinarily, they are not regarded as merely untrained in employeeship skills.

To remove worker ineffectiveness as a source of workplace conflict, leaders must provide training that's specifically directed at that purpose. At this time workers aren't trained in employeeship. Most workplace training, approximately ninety-five percent, is targeted at management and leadership training.

The other five percent is toward technical training for workers. No funds are spent on employeeship training for workers.

If leadership training is important to increase the value of leaders, certainly employeeship training should occupy some level of importance in productivity enhancement of workers.

Most productivity is accomplished through employeeship, not through leadership. It's doubtful that even the most well-trained leaders can effectively lead workers who aren't trained in employeeship toward maximum productivity, without workplace conflict. It's not only doubtful, for that situation exists today. Most workplaces now suffer from conflict that restricts optimum productivity.

Employeeship is analyzed in Chapter Four. For specific training purposes, however, leaders should conduct formal and informal training on the following subjects, as a minimum curriculum:

Authority and responsibility

Why productivity is important

Leadership alternatives

Personal development

Company goals and personal goals

The importance of each person

Workplace facts versus workplace myths

Personal accountability for individual success

Success planning

This is not the complete list of possible topics that may be presented, but these topics are critical and give examples of appropriate subjects. A summary of success planning will be discussed next.

Success Planning

Success planning is identified above as one of the requirements of good employeeship. Success planning hasn't been discussed in detail in this book; however, the concepts of success planning are simple enough to be understood by anyone, with only a basic outline of its requirements.

Success planning has two dimensions. One is individual

success planning for personal success. The other dimension concerns success planning to develop and maintain a harmonious workplace that emphasizes optimum productivity. Individual success planning will be reviewed first.

Personal Success Planning

If a person fails to become successful, or if a person feels he or she hasn't been successful enough to deserve self-esteem and pride, little can be done for that person to eliminate his or her feelings of frustration and alienation. These feeling of frustration and alienation are ordinarily reflected as conflict in the workplace.

At this time, individual success planning is a concept that's unknown by most workers and leaders. It's absence continues to perpetuate workplace conflict. Leaders must teach personal success planning to their workers to allow those workers to find self-worth and esteem for themselves. This esteem will force themselves to become motivated toward success. A successful worker creates a successful workplace.

A self-motivated worker who understands the purpose for that motivation requires less leadership to be productive. Less worker acquiescence and less leader encroachment into the conflict zone decreases that conflict. The following topics should be considered in that training process:

- How to set goals
- How to develop a success attitude
- How to solve problems
- How to analyze mistakes
- How to remain determined
- How to avoid peer pressure
- How to overcome success obstacles

This training will teach a worker how to develop a success pattern, how to develop increasing confidence, how to avoid obstacles to success and how to multiply little successes into a major success. A success plan may also be developed for a workplace. That will be discussed next.

Workplace Success Planning

Workplace success planning is similar to personal success planning. The difference is that the target of success is the goal of the workplace, not the goal of any individual. Workplace success planning requires emphasis in the following areas:

Clear goals must be established and understood by all members of the workplace.

Each member must have clear responsibilities that directly relate to quantity and quality toward that goal.

Each member should understand the circle of success and be confident in other members.

Each member should understand how the zone of conflict occurs.

The organization should strive for a relationship factor of a thousand, described in Chapter Ten.

Organizational success planning emphasizes individual competence, confidence, trust, and mutual anticipation that each person will fulfill his or her duties and responsibilities. Although this concept might seem similar to popular participative management concepts, it's not.

Participative programs emphasize team effort and team decision-making, and to some degree, attempts to use positive peer pressure. Success planning allows and encourages each person to maintain his or her own identity, to develop personal self-esteem and motivation, and to understand the reason for achieving company goals.

The major difference, however, is that participative management traditionally attempts to focus full attention and efforts on company goals. Success planning maintains that same focus on company goals, but also encourages the rights of individual workers to focus on personal self-development goals that may not be the same as company goals.

Social Pressures

Direct social pressures and indirect social influences cause many complications and frustrations to the processes of leadership, motivation, employeeship, and productivity. All these processes are essential not only to maintain harmony within the workplace, but also to solve many of those problems those same negative social pressures are designed to correct. In effect, many of those social demands on the workplace to solve social problems actually make those problems worse.

For example, is it better for our society to insure workplaces are racially and ethnically balanced; or, would a more rational solution be to help business leaders increase productivity to a level that would increase demand for more workers, including everbody who can work? Current social and governmental policies are oriented toward making internal business decisions rather than decisions that will contribute to the economic success of our country.

Our social solutions to solve economic problems, which really cause many of those social problems, are focused on symptoms rather than focused on fundamental problems. Most probably, enough economic expansion would solve most social problems. For example,

World War Two brought more women into the national workforce, because they were needed; they became an important part of our national success. Inappropriate social solutions will continue to frustrate the economic incentive.

Economic expansion cannot occur without governmental and social support of that expansion. Presently, that support is focused on survival politics and satisfaction of special interest groups rather than being focused on economic expansion.

The question might be asked, "How does this discussion on social influences relate to workplace conflict, and what can I do about it?" The purpose for this discussion is not to offer solutions to that question; even the great minds of the world haven't determined that answer. The purpose for this discussion on those negative social influences is to create awareness.

Leaders and workers should become aware of the insidiousness and the consequences of these influences upon their feelings and their actions in the workplace. With this awareness and this understanding, and with a mutual desire for workplace harmony, much of their frustration and despair may be directed at the proper source - negative social imposition - and not at each other.

A better understanding of mutual interests, mutual problems, and mutual negative forces will allow a more conducive atmosphere of mutual trust and confidence in the workplace. Without mutual trust and confidence, conflict will continue to be the great destroyer of productivity in the work environment.

Conclusion

This analysis of workplace conflict causes and consequences hasn't been made merely to help make workplaces happier places for workers and leaders. That condition would be a bonus for members of the work environment, but that condition may also exist in workplaces that aren't productive. The purpose for this analysis is to help reduce conflict that produces blatant or subtle anti-productivity feelings and activities in workplaces.

Management experts suggest that the level of real worker productivity is about fifty percent of worker capability. If this belief is only partially valid, then productivity may be increased by fifteen to twenty-five percent before a valid charge of worker exploitation may be made. This suggests a worker could use from sixty-five to seventy-five percent of his or her capability without discomfort.

The information is this book is designed to help leaders and workers capture that idle and discretionary fifteen to twenty-five percent of lost effort. One goal is to increase industrial productivity so industry may expand the economy to create more opportunities for personal success; this means more jobs.

Another goal is to increase self-reliance by workers so they understand they must create their own success; not wait for their workplaces to do that for them.

From the perspective of either a leader or a worker, in our zeal to succeed, we often forget that others must succeed to permit and support our success.

REFERENCED BIBLIOGRAPHY

Abraham H. Maslow, Motivation and Personality (Harper and Row, New York, 1954)

Douglas McGregor, The Human Side of Enterprise (McGraw-Hill Book Co., Inc., New York, 1960) Chap. 4

Douglas McGregor, The Human Side of Enterprise (McGraw-Hill Book Co., Inc., New York, 1960) Chap. 3

J. Jay Braun, Darwyn E. Linder, Isaac Asimov, Psychology Today: An Introduction (Random House, New York, 1979)

Frederick Herzberg, et el, The Motivation to Work (John Wiley and Sons, New York, 1959)

Robert L. Kahn and Daniel Katz, Leadership Practices in Relation to Productivity and Morale (From Group Dynamics, Research and Theory by Darwin Cartwright and Alvin Zander, Harper and Rowe Publishers, 1960)

Robert Schuller, Move Ahead With Possibility Thinking (Fleming H. Revell Co., Old Tappan, NJ, 1978)

Alfred J. Marrow, Behind the Executive Mask (American Management Association, no. 79, New York, 1964)

James H. Donnelly, Jr., James L. Gibson, John M. Ivancevich, Fundamentals of Management (Business Publications, Inc., Austin, TX, 1971) Chap. 10.

Robert Tannenbaum and Warren H. Schmidt, "How to Choose a Leadership Pattern," Harvard Business Review, vol. 36, pp. 95-101, March-April, 1958.

Robert R. Blake and Jane Mouton, The Managerial Grid (Houston, TX: Gulf Publ., 1964)

James H. Donnelly, Jr., James L. Gibson, John M. Ivancevich, Fundamentals of Management (Business Publications, Inc., Austin, TX, 1971) Pg. 196.

Clifford T. Morgan, Introduction to Psychology (McGraw Hill Book Co., Inc., New York, 1956)

Soloman E. Asch, Opinions and Social Pressure, Scientific American, vol. 193, no. 5, pp 31-35, Nov., 1955.

L.C. Dunn and Theodosius Dobzhansky, Heredity, Race and Society (The New American Library, New York, NY, 1960)

Michael B. Katz, In the Shadow of the Poorhouse (Basic Books, Inc., New York, 1986)

C. Northgate Parkinson and Nigel Rowe, Communicate (Prentice Hall International, Englewood Cliffs, NJ, 1978)

ADDITIONAL BIBLIOGRAPHY

Ken Auletta, The Underclass (Vintage Books, NY, 1982)

Bernard Berelson and Gary Steiner, Human Behavior (Brace and World, Inc., New York, 1967)

Joseph R. Blasi, Employee Ownership (Harper & Row, NY, 1988)

John Chancellor, Perils and Promises (Harper & Row, NY, 1990)

Lester Coch and John French, Jr., Overcoming Resistance to Change, Human Relations, Vol. 4, no. 1, pp. 512-533, 1948.

Commerce Clearing House, Inc., 1987 Guide to Labor Relations.

Olga L. Crocker, Syril Charney, Johnny Sik Leung Chiu; Quality Circles (Mentor Books, NY, 1984)

James H. Davis, Group Performance (Addison-Wesley Publ. Co., Reading, MA, 1969.

Stanley M. Davis, Managing Corporate Cultures (Harper & Row, Publ., NY, 1984)

Max DePree, Leadership is an Art (Dell Publ., NY, 1989)

Michael L. Dertouzos, Richard K. Lester, Robert M. Solow; Made in America (Harper Perennial Books, NY, 1989)

Peter Drucker, Management: Tasks, Responsibilities, Practices (Harper and Row Publ., New York, 1974)

Peter Drucker, The New Realities (Harper & Row, Publ., NY, 1989)
Diane Fassel, Working Ourselves to Death (Harper San Francisco, CA, 1990)

Wendell L. French, Fremont E. Kast, James E. Rosenzweig; Understanding Human Behavior in Organizations (Harper & Row, Publ., NY, 1985)

Richard Hodgetts and Donald F. Kuratko, Management (Harcourt Brace Jovanovich, Publ., NY, 1988)

George P. Huber, Motivation and Competence, Academy of Management Journal, vol. 10, no. 3, pp. 275-285, Sept., 1967

Gerald Jackson, Executive ESP (Pocket Books, NY, 1989)

Mark H. McCormack, What They Still Don't Teach You at the Harvard Business School (Bantam Books, NY, 1989)

Lawrence M. Miller, Barbarians to Bureaucrats (Ballantine Books, NY, 1989)

Patrick Montana and Bruce Charnov, Management (Barron's,1987)

John Naisbitt and Patricia Aburdene, Re-inventing the Corporation (Warner Books, NY, 1985)

Thomas J. Peters and Robert H. Waterman, Jr., In Search of Excellence (Warner Books, NY, 1982)

Frances Fox Pivens and Richard A. Cloward, Poor People's Movements (Vintage Books, NY, 1979)

Clyde Prestowitz, Jr., Trading Places (Bantam Books, Inc., NY, 1989)

Kenneth Schatz and Linda Schatz, Managing by Influence (Prentice-Hall, Englewood Cliffs, NJ, 1986)

Paul M. Stokes, Total Job Training (American Management Association, NY, 1966)

Clarence C. Walton, The Moral Manager (Harper & Row, NY, 1988)

Abraham Zaleznik, The Managerial Mystique (Harper & Row, NY, 1989)

Managing The Conflict Zone

About the Author

Will Clark is a retired military officer. He served six years as an enlisted person before earning his commission through the last class of Air Force Officer Candidate School, in 1963.

During his military career he served in many worker, manager, and staff positions, and in many countries. He completed major management and leadership schools in the military, including: Officer Candidate School, Squadron Officers School and Air Command and Staff College. During that time he earned a degree in management and business from the University of Nebraska. He also taught business courses for the City Colleges of Chicago. After his military service, he was a manager in industry for the next twelve years.

He is now a writer and a management and motivational consultant, and the founder of Motivation Basics, a consulting firm that provides motivational training for employees and high school students. He also provides management and leadership training.

He has authored five other motivation and leadership books. They are: *Who's Blaming Who? Simply Success, The Leadership Handbook, How to Learn,* and *In Search of Education.*

For more current information about the author and his books, visit:

AuthorsDen.com